RACE, RELIGION & RACISM

RACE, RELIGION & RACISM

Volume One

A Bold Encounter With Division in the Church

Frederick K.C. Price

FAITH ONE PUBLISHING

Faith One Publishing
Los Angeles, California

4th Printing

Race, Religion & Racism, Volume One
Perverting the Gospel to Subjugate a People
ISBN 10: 1-883798-81-7
ISBN 13: 978-1-883798-81-9
Library of Congress Catalog Card Number: 99-75670

P.O. Box 90000
Los Angeles, CA 90009
Published by Faith One Publishing
7901 South Vermont Avenue
Los Angeles, California 90044

Publisher's Cataloging-in-Publication
(Provided by Quality Books, Inc.)

Price, Frederick K.C.
Race, religion & racism, a bold encounter with division in the church Vol. I / by Frederick K.C. Price -- 1st ed.
p.cm.

Includes bibliographical references and index.
LCCN: 99-75670
ISBN: 1-883798-48-5

1. Race relations--Religious aspects--Christianity. 2. Racism--Religious aspects--Christianity. 3. Race--Religious aspects--Christianity. 4. Race--Biblical teaching.
I. Title.

BT734.2.P75 2001 261.8'348
QBI00-500153

Dedication

It would have been difficult for me to complete
Race, Religion & Racism
—both the television series and this book—
without the rock-solid support of my family.

I dedicate this book to them:
my wife of 46 years
Betty R. Price;
our daughters and sons-in-law
Angela M. Evans and her husband, A. Michael Evans, Jr.,
Cheryl A. Crabbe and her husband, Allen L. Crabbe, Jr.,
and Stephanie P. Buchanan and her husband, Danon R. Buchanan;
our son
Frederick K. Price;
and our grandchildren
Alan and Adrian Evans,
Nicole and Allen Crabbe, III,
and Tyler Buchanan.

—Frederick K.C. Price

Table of Contents

Foreword

As this is being written, our nation is searching its soul for rational explanations to the various hate crimes that daily dominate our news. We are shocked by the trend of random acts of violence and hate, but yet we turn a blind eye to the most prevalent hate crime around us: racism against blacks. While we, as a society, will openly discuss gender, religious, class or sexual orientation and even ethnic issues, we still refuse to discuss race or racism for fear of destroying the myth of racial harmony. It is this hypocrisy and indifference toward issues of race, as well as the continued hostile feelings toward black people, that underlie and fuel most of our nation's smoldering hate crimes.

But it is time for change. As ignorant as our society has remained about the roots of racism that continue to plague those of color and degenerate our society, there is hope because there is a cure: knowledge. This book contains such knowledge—the knowledge to set *all* men free, whether they are black, white, brown, red, or yellow.

And there is hope in that God alone has uniquely raised up just the man needed to expose the ugly truth of racism: Dr. Frederick K.C. Price. Dr. Price is indeed the man of the hour, for his teaching on race, religion and racism is right on time. In fact, it is essential to the weeding out of racism in our society, which must happen before racial harmony can become a reality.

As someone who is dedicated to the education and uplifting of black people, it is a privilege and an honor for me to know such a man of integrity as Dr. Price. He has risked much by taking a stand and teaching on the overt and not-so-overt racism that he sees throughout the Church. Despite the many great personal achievements that have elevated him to a more privileged position in life — building the largest church sanctuary in the nation totally debt-free, being honored with both a Horatio Alger Award and the SCLC's Kelly Miller Interfaith Award, teaching for more than 20 consecutive years on national television, and founding one this nation's largest churches — he has never forgotten from whence he came. Nor has he forsaken his desire to help others prosper in the things of God so that their lives are enriched.

That is why, after years of research and study, Dr. Price launched the teaching series *Race, Religion & Racism* over his internationally televised *Ever Increasing Faith* television program. This series has had a major impact. Like the watchman sitting on the tower warning the people, Dr. Price systematically revealed the discrepancy between what is church practice and what is biblical Scripture. In so doing, he has exposed the role organized religion played in the enslavement of black people and the subsequent maintenance of the structural racism that has laid a foundation for social disharmony in America.

Race, Religion & Racism has sounded the alarm against the continued maltreatment of an entire group of people who, according to the Bible, God clearly recognizes as instrumental to His plan and purpose for mankind. It has helped to awaken our nation and the world to the reality that black people have made a contribution, that we have made a difference, and that it is time for us to truly reap the benefits of the contributions we have made.

Race, Religion & Racism is also a call to action. Its purpose is not to exalt people of color above or against any other group of people, but to encourage them to have their own best interests at heart in terms of how they treat, look at, and work with one another. For this Word from God, I for one am grateful.

I thank God that Dr. Price has allowed himself to be used as a catalyst for change. Those who have ears to hear this message will at last receive accurate knowledge that can empower them to institute the changes that are needed. But change must first begin with how we view ourselves and then in how we view others in light of ourselves. And this, too, is a revelation that Dr. Price has brought forth. This book truly is a guide for those who want to have their spiritual life in order. It will help those who practice racism in ignorance, as well as those who do it purposefully.

Foreword

What you hold in your hand is very special and powerful. This book, *Race, Religion & Racism*, reveals the long distance that religion has traveled from the moment the first humans appeared in Africa's garden of Eden. And more poignantly, it reveals the great distance it has to travel before it can bind us into the most important race of all: the human race.

—Dr. Claud Anderson

President of The Harvest Institute
Author of: *Black Labor, White Wealth*
Dirty Little Secrets About Black History
and *PowerNomics*

Preface

Race, Religion & Racism is the culmination of five years' work, forty-five years as a minister, and a lifetime as a black man. The seed for it was planted when God gave me an assignment to teach on the subject of racism in the Church. Several years later, a personal incident occurred that served as an additional catalyst. What followed were three years of research, during which I pored over numerous magazine and newspaper articles, scores of popular and scholarly books, as well as letters, tapes and websites. In October 1997, I began to deliver the message as a series on my *Ever Increasing Faith* television program. This book is based on those teachings.

Part One of this volume discusses the personal incident that catalyzed me to fulfill my assignment, and presents an overview of race, religion and racism in America. Part Two is a detailed analysis of why racism is wrong from both a biblical and a scientific perspective, and how and why racism has been encouraged and tolerated in this country. Part Two also traces America's attitude toward Blacks, from the introduction of slavery until today. It points out the effects of those attitudes on black people and suggests what may be done to make amends for the past.

Put in its most basic terms, the purpose of this book is to expose racism in the Church and in our country for the sin that it is.

Acknowledgments

First, thanks to my heavenly Father; my Savior and Lord Jesus Christ, the head of the Church; and the Holy Spirit, who gave the inspiration for this project. I was merely a willing vessel.

Few people can fully appreciate or understand all the work that goes into producing and marketing a book of this magnitude. There are typists, editors, researchers, printers, artists, publicists, marketing people, advertising people, attorneys and others. Though I thank them all, several special people should be mentioned by name:

Of course, I must acknowledge the love and support of my mother Winifred Price and my sister Delores Price.

Next, I want to express my love and appreciation to the staff of Faith One Publishing, our excellent in-house book-publishing staff: Director Stanley O. Williford, editor-writers Jonathan Yungkans, Pat Hays and Julianne Nachtrab; writer Martha Tucker, and secretary Rose Brown.

I want to note the fine work of editors Mark Rosin and Cynthia Hoppenfeld-Rosin, who did a tremendous job on the final editing of this book. Likewise, I thank copy editor Nitza Wilon for a masterful job.

I am also deeply grateful for the work of research assistant Cheryl Bennett, indexer Victoria Agee, transcriptionist Doris Pettigrew and typesetter Maggy Graham. Without the efforts of these ladies, the book would have lacked many of the extra enhancements that make it both easy to read and useful for study.

For the cover and graphic effects, I must acknowledge the superb work of the Art Department staff: Director Keni Davis, Manager James E. Brown and artists Jeff Burns, Claretta G. Rainey and Lonnie Ratcliff.

Our Media Department is a constant source of pride. Under the direction of former Director A. Michael Evans Jr. (now vice president, marketing) and Christopher B. Gregory, manager of video and audio, they have performed expertly in keeping the book before the eyes of our television viewers.

Public Relations, Advertising Director Corliss M. Williford and her assistants, Delphine Nelson and Belinda Bolden, deserve praise for their efforts in promotion and advertising. We also acknowledge the suggestions of former Marketing Director B. Michael Coleman, as well as the input of Special Assistant Ranada Palmer.

Finance Director Beverly Conley did a fine job of shepherding the project fiscally.

Thanks are also due the Faith One Publishing sales staff, headed by Account Executive Danon R. Buchanan, and sales representatives Marcus Andrews and Jennifer Brown.

Gregg Ketter of the Ketter Group must be highly commended for his work in pulling together various sales, advertising, publicity and printing elements for the book.

The Executive Board of Crenshaw Christian Center stood solidly behind me when the *Race, Religion & Racism* series began. Much love and appreciation are due Mrs. Angela M. Evans, Mrs. Cheryl A. Crabbe, Pastor James E. Price, Pastor L. Craig Hays, (former member, Pastor Milt Jackson), Dr. Alfonza Stakley, Dr. Edward Holden, Dr. William Williams, Anthony Ramos, Harvey Cloyd, Ronald Whitaker and Jennette Fant.

I had the same demonstration of loving support from my assistant pastors: L. Craig Hays, James E. Price, Allen J. Landry, Garry D. Zeigler, (former CCC pastor, Milt Jackson), Gilbert Burns, Mark A. McVay, Mike Reid, (former pastoral assistant, Argie Taylor), and pastoral assistants, Betty R. Price and Delores Price.

We should never underestimate the value of loyalty and faithfulness. As such, I give honor to those Directors of the Fellowship of Inner City Word of Faith Ministries (FICWFM) who stuck by me: Dr. Ira V. Hilliard, Dr. Sammie Holloway, Dr. David M. Copeland, Pastor Charles Brown, Dr. Kevin B. Brewer, Dr. Arthur J. Aragon, Pastor Michael A. Freeman, Dr. Alfred D. Harvey Jr., Dr. James A.

Kuykendall, Pastor Wiley Jackson Jr. and Pastor Donald Shorter Sr., and, of course, all of the faithful members of FICWFM.

Of my friends in ministry, three stand out: My "son" in the ministry, Dr. Hilliard, for his bold and courageous stand when others forsook me, and for taking time from his own television program to air a statement backing me all the way; also Dr. John A. Cherry and Bishop Charles E. Blake, who were strong and godly sources of support during the series.

I am grateful for the support of such renowned men of God as Oral Roberts and his wife Evelyn, as well as Terry Mize. Their encouragement was especially important against the silence of so many others.

My friend, educator, political strategist and businessman, Dr. Claud Anderson, was and is a wellspring of information and inspiration. I express my immense gratitude to him.

Thank you, Dr. Jean Perez, for your prayers.

Attorneys Roger P. Furey, Freya L. Christian, and Norma J. Williams of the law firm of Arter & Hadden, LLP, are to be commended for their incisive advice and legal wisdom.

Kudos to Senior Sales Representative Jamie Butcher of RR Donnelley & Sons for his expert advice in the printing of this book.

And how can I ever forget those thousands of *Ever Increasing Faith* viewers and Faith Partners, many of whom sent notices of support by phone, e-mail and letter, or expressed them to me face to face? May the Lord richly reward and bless every one of you for your kindness to me and my family.

Finally, to the congregation of Crenshaw Christian Center, one word — Awesome! You are the best congregation in the whole world.

To these and all those who have assisted in any way with the production of this book, I thank you and remind you of the promise so graciously given to you by our heavenly Father in Hebrews 6:10:

> **God is not unjust to forget your work and labor of love which you have shown toward His name, in that you have ministered to the saints, and do minister.**

Part One

1

My Assignment From God

When I came into the world in Santa Monica, California, in the early 1930s, it was primarily a white city. There was a small, roughly eight-block-square area where most of the black people lived. Although there was a scattering of Blacks in other parts of town, there were areas where black people did not go. In fact, we could not go to the beach of our choice; we had to go to a certain section about a block wide that had been set aside for black people. We could not go to the right or to the left; we had to go to that one section.

As a kid, I was very curious, so I asked a lot of questions. I couldn't understand why black people could not live beyond a particular boulevard, why it was all white in one area and all black in another. I couldn't understand why there were black churches and white churches and Hispanic churches in different parts of the city, each church serving only one ethnic group. No one seemed to have an answer. They said, "Well, that's the way it's always been." I certainly didn't know, so I accepted it.

I was not brought up in what you would call a Christian home. Some of the friends I palled around with had parents who went to church, so I heard biblical names here and there and certain phrases like, "Jesus is the way," but that was the extent of my spiritual awareness.

When I was 21, I met a young lady named Betty Ruth Scott, who was a Christian and 19 at the time. I went to church with her while we were courting because I was trying to make points, and I wanted her and her parents to think that I was a nice guy. I was, but I was a nice heathen. Her church did not really teach from the Bible, so she did not know, from a biblical perspective, that she should not have been involved with me. Thank God He helps us when we don't know—it's when we know and will not do that we are cut off from God's help.

Shortly after Betty and I married, I became born-again. I accepted Jesus Christ as my personal Savior and Lord at a tent revival meeting and was taken to the counseling area, where people were given instructions about the decision they had made to receive Christ and what it meant to live for Him. The majority of the people who were there that night were white, and only two or three of us were black. My counselor was a white man, a minister of the Gospel. He was also a teacher in one of the Bible colleges in Los Angeles, and had a daily radio broadcast teaching the Word of God.

He asked me why I responded to the invitation, and I told him what had happened to me as I heard the Gospel preached. He explained Christ's sacrifice to me, then asked if I had any questions, and, of course, I did. I said, "I don't understand how this Jesus whom I've just received is the way, the truth and the life, and how He's the answer to all of humanity's problems, and yet everything about Him is racially segregated. Is heaven going to be like that? Is there going to be a segregated heaven?"

He took the Bible and showed me from the Scriptures—interpreting them in his own way—that it was God's will for the races to be separated. I did not know it then, but this was my introduction to the way the Bible has been twisted and distorted by one group to the detriment of another. How many generations of Blacks have believed that they are cursed and inferior to the rest of mankind because of the so-called curse of Ham, a corrupted teaching of the Bible that has been traditionally propounded by certain Christians?[1]

Black people in America have been taught to believe that the white man has all the answers and that black people know nothing. At that time, I figured that this counselor must know what he was telling me. Number one, he was white; number two, he was a minister of the Gospel; number three, he had a radio broadcast; and number four, he was a teacher in a Bible institute. So I accepted what he said. I did not like it, but I accepted it because it seemed to make sense, and history certainly seemed to back him up.

He encouraged me to join a church. Since my wife was from a Baptist background, we went to a Baptist church. I joined, and a short time later I had a divine encounter. There is a story in the Bible found in the ninth chapter of the Book of Acts, in which Paul was on his way to Damascus when a bright light shone around him and he fell to the ground and heard a voice speaking to him; it was the voice of Jesus. I had a similar experience. I did not see a light and I did not fall, but I definitely heard the voice of Jesus speaking to me.

At that time, I did not know who it was, because I had no Bible knowledge. Since then, as I've read the Old Testament, I have read many times how the prophets would say, "... and the Word of the Lord came to me saying ..." or "... thus saith the Lord...." That day, the Word of the Lord came to me saying….

---

[1] I will discuss the myth of the curse of Ham in Part Two of this volume, Chapters 5 and 7. Also see Robert E. Hood, *Begrimed and Black: Christian Traditions on Blacks and Blackness* (Minneapolis: Fortress Press, 1994), 115-131. Hood, a professor of religious studies and director of the Center of African-American Studies at Adelphi University, explains how long the myth of the Hamitic curse has existed and reports that early scholars such as Martin Luther (1483-1546) debated its validity. He also reports on the internalized oppression among some Blacks who believed the myth themselves.

I do not mean that a thought passed through my mind; I mean that I heard what to me was an audible voice. I did not see anyone, but the voice had direction to it. It came from over my left shoulder. I thought someone was talking to me from that part of the building, so I turned to see who it was, but there was no one there—nothing but the choir stand, and on Sunday nights the stand was empty. But the voice I heard was just as distinct, just as loud, just as real as if I heard it from someone talking to me from across a table.

The voice said, "You are to preach My Gospel." That was my call to the ministry.

From 1955 to 1970, Betty and I went through several denominations trying to find a church home. In 1970, I received the baptism with the Holy Spirit with the evidence of speaking with other tongues, according to Acts 2:4. My whole perception of the Bible dramatically changed, and the teaching gift was dropped into my spirit. From that point on, all I wanted to do was teach the Word of God. I did not have much Bible knowledge then, so I taught the bits and pieces that I had, and as I gave myself to the study of the Bible, that knowledge increased.

Again I was confronted with racial prejudice and I did not like it. It seemed to me that there should be a spiritual level to which one would rise where ethnicity would not matter, where people's color would be irrelevant and immaterial. But I was rudely awakened to find out that regardless of how high some people go spiritually, they can still have enormous and devastating blind spots, because they do not permit their spiritual knowledge to affect their feelings or beliefs when it comes to people of other cultures.

I personally believe that the subjects of race, religion and racism have not been adequately dealt with in the Church of the Lord Jesus Christ. I am going to deal with these subjects in ways I have never heard them dealt with before. I have been researching this book for about three years. I may appear angry, but my anger is a holy anger that is scripturally based. It is not anger against an individual person or group of persons, so whatever the color of your skin, as you read this book, I do not want you to feel intimidated.

In America, our biggest problem with racism has been the black and white issue. To get to the bottom of it and come up with a solution, we are going to have to look at the facts as they really are, not as they have been painted by the media and by others who do not really want to deal with the subject truthfully. In discussing it, I am going to be using the words *white people*, *black people*, *Black*, *White*, *African American* and *Negro*; I will also be using the word *nigger*, because unfortunately that word has been used by some people in this country for hundreds of years. I am not doing this to offend anyone, but simply to present the situation as it really is.

Most racial problems have historical roots. You did not start racism and I did not start it, but we are now living with its consequences. Much of what is going on today is occurring because most people are ignorant of the facts and unclear about the origins of racism. If you do not know how something started, you cannot fix it. That is why we have to go back to the beginning in order to deal effectively with the problems of race and racism.

In my own life, something happened to me that was very traumatic, and God used it to awaken me to the realization that racial prejudice is alive and, unfortunately, doing quite well in the Church today. In the late 1980s, God had given me the assignment to teach on race, religion and racism. I knew in my spirit this was something I had to do, but to be truthful about it, I had been dragging my feet. After all, who wants to deal with this sensitive issue in a public forum? That traumatic event became the catalyst for me to prepare this teaching.

2

Symptoms of the Problem

Shortly after I was given the assignment, I received this letter:

Dear Pastor Price,

I hope you actually get to read this letter yourself and not a secretary who reads this and then responds with another computer-generated letter.

In May, I attended the West Coast Believer's Convention in Anaheim, California. You preached on "Faith Worketh by Love." Pastor Price, I need to ask you to forgive me for not loving you. I did not love you because of your skin color. I did not want to listen to you because of your skin color. In all actuality, I hated you simply because of your skin color. I asked the Lord to forgive me. I know I have been forgiven of my bigotry from the Lord. But Pastor Price, I would also like to know that you have forgiven me as well. It would be greatly appreciated.

You also prayed at the end of your message for us as a body to receive prosperity, promotions at work, etc. I cannot remember the rest of the prayer. Anyways, I

> wanted you to know that I just received a promotion at work. Along with the promotion came an increase in pay. Praise the Lord! Thank you, Pastor Price, for praying that prayer.
>
> Thank you for your time and your consideration. I'm looking forward to hearing from you at your earliest convenience.
>
> Your brother in Christ,
> [Name withheld][1]

Obviously, I forgave the brother. I could not be a Christian and hold something against the man. I knew he did it out of ignorance, but he asked my forgiveness and I gave it to him.

That was 1990. I saved the letter because I had a sense that it would help me in fulfilling my assignment. It is symptomatic of the racial situation in America. So are several letters from *Charisma* magazine, responding to an article entitled, "When Love Crosses the Color Line."[2] One of these is illustrative of the basic point of view held by many white Christians:

> I am highly offended by your articles on interracial marriage. *It is wrong to marry out of your race* [italics added for emphasis]. Jesus knows this, *since it lowers the physical standard in races*, what about the offspring?
>
> [Name withheld][3]

Another letter writer commented:

---

[1] For the most part, throughout this book, in order to protect the privacy of the individuals involved, their names are not revealed.

[2] Letters to the Editor, *Charisma*, v. 21, no. 1 (August 1995), 8.

[3] *Charisma*, 8.

> I was so disappointed when I received your July issue promoting interracial marriage. And if that wasn't bad enough, you said Moses married a Negro.
>
> If you'd take the time to study your history, you'd see that there were different races in Midian at different times. What you published is just another lie.
>
> *We marry after our own kind if we want to be pleasing to God* [italics added for emphasis]. May God open your eyes and show you the truth.
>
> [Name withheld][4]

I guess the person who wrote this has never read Numbers 12, in which the Bible says that Moses had married an Ethiopian woman. This letter-writer's misinformation, as well as the prejudice that underlies it, is part of the problem that we are facing in America. And it has been the problem since the inception of this nation.

Notice what she said about *Charisma* in reference to Moses marrying a Negro: "What you published is just another lie. We marry after our own kind if we want to be pleasing to God." See how God is interwoven into people's personal and individual prejudices?

Let me tell you what I mean when I use the word *racism*, so you will understand my position. For now, I want to focus on racial, ethnic and color prejudice, terms that are encompassed under the general term *racism*. Most of the time, when people say "racism," they mean racial prejudice. When we talk about racism and racial prejudice in America, we are usually referring to the situation between Blacks and Whites. Of course, it occurs in other segments of society, too, but the black and white issue in America is predominant.

---

[4] *Charisma*, 8

In the second letter, we get an inkling of the racial issue when the writer talks about how we should "marry after our own kind if we want to be pleasing to God"; the first letter-writer asks, "...what about the offspring?"

This is the issue nobody wants to deal with directly: the fact that America is permeated with the idea that black people are genetically inferior.[5] I do not care about interracial marriage as such—I am neither for it, nor against it—but I have to deal with it because it is the big hang-up that most white people have concerning black people. *Blacks are inferior; therefore, their blood has to be inferior.*

When this lie was first forged in this country, many Whites thought that the disposition of a person, his quality, his character was transmitted through the blood, because at the time, there was no understanding of genetics. So if you mix white blood and black blood, since black blood is inferior, and white blood is superior, then you will taint the white blood, and it will no longer be pure. Based on that proposition, we have to keep the races apart.[6]

Returning to the assertion that it was a lie that Moses married a Negro, the Bible says in Numbers 12:1:

> **Then Miriam and Aaron spoke against Moses because of the Ethiopian woman whom he had married; for he had married an Ethiopian woman.**

Ethiopia is on the continent of Africa, not Europe. Its people are black. Moses, the Bible tells us, married an Ethiopian, and if you read carefully, you will see that God did not say anything about it one

---

[5] I will be introducing more information that was used by doctors attempting to validate this idea in Part Two, Chapter 11.

[6] Indeed, as we will see in Part Two, segregation of the races in America, like racism itself, was actually based on economics. See George M. Fredrickson, *White Supremacy: A Comparative Study in American & South African History* (New York: Oxford University Press, 1981), 68.

way or another. In fact, Aaron and Miriam criticized Moses for it, and God struck Miriam with leprosy. Moses was God's man, and yet it says right there in the Bible that "he had married an Ethiopian woman."

Again, I am not promoting interracial marriages, but the reactions to the *Charisma* article are important expressions of people's underlying racial attitudes. Many white people in America were taught racial bigotry by their parents and forebears, and it has been perpetrated through time—often subliminally. It isn't always announced with big neon signs, but the message is clear.

Apparently, however, interracial marriage was all right with God, because He did not chastise Moses for marrying a black woman.

3

What the Church Has Allowed

I received a suggestion from a fellow minister to call a phone number and listen to the following recorded message:

> White pride! White man, fight back. If you've been watching the news lately, you've heard that there is evidence of the CIA bringing cocaine into the U.S. and funneling it into Niggertown to raise money for the rebels in Nicaragua. In plain English, the government made drugs available for niggers—drugs, which make the niggers more violent and dangerous. It would be like the CIA injecting animals with rabies and turning them loose in our communities. The government is so corrupt and evil, one wonders how much longer God's wrath upon America will be withheld. When you take primitive, emotional creatures likes Negroes and dope them up, you create a dangerous, violent, criminal animal that robs and kills for crack money. CIA's scumbag and scumbags like Lt. Col. Oliver North, who seems to have been in on the CIA's drug-running operation, should be put on trial for treason. On top of all of that, we have Clinton, a president who supports a form of abortion which kills a baby as it's being born by sucking its brain out and crushing the skull. If anyone did that to a dog, the whole country would be outraged. The president is evil and corrupt. Vote scumbag Clinton out in 1996. Vote

> for Dole; at least Dole is against killing babies.... This is [name withheld], reminding you that it's all right to be white. Please note our new area code is 561. This hot line does not record incoming messages. New message every week. White power!

Notice how this recording talks about the "niggers"? It even refers to "Niggertown." White supremacists are not the only ones who do this, they are just the only ones who have the guts to come out in the open and say it. I have to respect them for that, even though I do not respect them for anything else. Their philosophy is evil, but at least they are not two-faced like the Church and some Christians.

This taped message tells us in no uncertain terms that there is a racial, ethnic and color problem in America, and it cannot be denied. That, by itself, is bad news indeed, but when you compound it with the fact that this racial, ethnic and color problem exists in the Church of the Lord Jesus Christ, it becomes a tragedy of enormous proportions. Why do I say that? Because in Matthew 5:13, it says:

> **"You are the salt of the earth...."**

And Verse 14 says:

> **"You are the light of the world...."**

The Church is supposed to be the salt of the earth. The Church is supposed to be the light of the world. Jesus said, we are **"the salt of the earth"**; He said, we are **"the light of the world...."**

Notice what Jesus did not say: Jesus did not say we are the salt of the Church; He did not say we are the light of the Church. He said we are the light of the world, and that is why the world and the society here in America are in such terrible trouble—because the Church is just as racist as the secular arena. The secular arena has no reason to clean up its act, because the Church is acting just like it.

We may have thought that Jesus meant we should be the taillight, but He actually meant we ought to be the headlight. He said, we are the *light*—which means we ought to be leading. We are giving the world a bad example because there is so much prejudice in the Church. That is why racism can exist in society the way it does.

It all started when the preachers got into league with the slave owners, and the Church sanctioned slavery. That is the reason slavery could exist—because the Church gave its approval for slave owners to practice slavery and call themselves Christians.[1] That is a major reason why many people of color have called Christianity the slave owners' or the white man's religion and have wanted nothing to do with it.

There were, of course, genuine Christians who spoke out against slavery. But slavery persisted in America for 246 years,[2] because the Church as a whole never committed itself to a positive program to end it.[3] Even since slavery ended, instead of taking on the racial, ethnic and color issues that face all humanity and dealing

---

1 See Oscar Reiss, *Blacks in Colonial America* (North Carolina: McFarland & Co., Inc., 1997), 17-21. Reiss reports that ministers such as Thomas Bacon openly taught their congregations that slavery was an institution sanctioned by God, and that black members were to be submissive and obedient because it was the will of God. Reiss further reports that black preachers could keep their positions as ministers as long as they, too, spoke in favor of slavery and obedience. Also see Emily Albu, J. William Frost, Howard Clark Kee, Carter Lindberg and Dana L. Robert, *Christianity: A Social and Cultural History* (New York: Prentice Hall, Inc., 1998), 448. After the American Revolution, the Baptists and Methodists threw out their opposition to slavery when they learned that preaching against it "doomed their expansion."

2 See Richard D. Brown and Stephen G. Rabe, eds., Slavery in American Society (Lexington, Massachusetts: D.C. Heath & Co., 1976), 3. Two hundred and forty-six years encompasses the arrival of the first Africans in America in 1619 through the end of the Civil War in 1865.

3 See Albu, Frost, Kee, Lindberg and Robert, 449-450. Referring to slavery, they write, "Major American denominations, fearing schisms, attempted to straddle the issue. Episcopalians, Lutherans, and Roman Catholics took no stand."

with them head-on from an unprejudiced, biblical perspective, the Church has acted as if the issues were not there. Historically and up to the present time, the Church has been a perfect example of the ostrich syndrome, hiding its head in the sand. That day is over. As 1 Peter 4:17 says:

> **For the time has come for judgment to begin at the house of God; and if it begins with us first, what will be the end of those who do not obey the gospel of God?**

Judgment Day has arrived. We are on the threshold of it now. We can no longer do business as usual. The attitude of the Christian toward racial, ethnic and color differences in mankind should be the same as God's.

The letters I quoted from *Charisma* condemned interracial marriages. Again, I am not advocating interracial marriage, but I want to bring out the underlying reason for racial strife. The real issue is the perception that black people are inferior and white people are superior. All the other issues—the name-calling (which white supremacists do in public and many other white people do in private), the hateful attitudes, and accusations of black violence and animalistic behavior—is a dodge; it is a way to avoid dealing with mixing the races.

The real issue is the belief that if you mix black and white blood, you are going to have a mongrel. As I said before, the Christian attitude toward racial, ethnic and color differences in mankind should be the same as God's, since we are supposed to be the children of God. Churches are supposed to be the churches of God. We are supposed to be the Body of Christ. Our attitude toward any ethnic group ought to be the same as God's. Doesn't that seem reasonable?

Maybe the problem with the Church is that it has never really found out how God thinks. What people have done is try to bring God down to their prejudiced level. But we have to bring the level of our ideas up to the level of God's. And if our ideas don't square with God, we are going to have to change them. As Christians, it is crucial for us to do this, because many people have turned away from Jesus because of what they have seen in the actions and attitudes of people who say they believe in God.

The reality of our Christianity has to be manifested in the way we treat each other. Everything I claim to believe as a Christian has to be lived out, and I cannot live it out on a desert island by myself. I have to live it out in interaction with you and you with me. How I act toward you and how you act toward me, how you see me, how I see you, these are the real bottom-line tests of the Christianity that we claim to live by.

And nothing makes our country's—and the Church's—failure of this test clearer than looking at how we view each other and comparing it to how the Bible tells us we should view each other.

4

How God Sees Humanity

God is the Creator. In the tenth chapter of Acts, there is a very revealing story about the Apostle Peter. Peter was a devout Jew. He was prejudiced against Gentiles, and did not think they could be saved, because he thought that Christ came only for Israel. Acts 10:9-23 tells us:

The next day, as they went on their journey and drew near the city, Peter went up on the housetop to pray, about the sixth hour.

Then he became very hungry and wanted to eat; but while they made ready, he fell into a trance

and saw heaven opened and an object like a great sheet bound at the four corners, descending to him and let down to the earth.

In it were all kinds of four-footed animals of the earth, wild beasts, creeping things, and birds of the air.

And a voice came to him, "Rise, Peter; kill and eat."

But Peter said, "Not so, Lord! For I have never eaten anything common or unclean."

And a voice spoke to him again the second time, "What God has cleansed you must not call common."

This was done three times. And the object was taken up into heaven again.

Now while Peter wondered within himself what this vision which he had seen meant, behold, the men who had been sent from Cornelius had made inquiry for Simon's house, and stood before the gate.

And they called and asked whether Simon, whose surname was Peter, was lodging there.

While Peter thought about the vision, the Spirit said to him, "Behold, three men are seeking you.

"Arise therefore, go down and go with them, doubting nothing; for I have sent them."

Then Peter went down to the men who had been sent to him from Cornelius, and said, "Yes, I am he whom you seek. For what reason have you come?"

And they said, "Cornelius the centurion, a just man, one who fears God and has a good reputation among all the nation of the Jews, was divinely instructed by a holy angel to summon you to his house, and to hear words from you."

Then he invited them in and lodged them. On the next day Peter went away with them, and some brethren from Joppa accompanied him.

Acts 10:9-23 tells us that through this experience, Peter opened himself to Gentiles for the first time without prejudice. Later, in Verses 10:34-35, we are told God's attitude toward ethnic groups:

> **Then Peter opened his mouth and said: "In truth I perceive that God shows no partiality.**
>
> **"But in every nation whoever fears Him and works righteousness is accepted by Him."**

I am quoting from the *New King James Version.*[1] The traditional *King James Version* says, **"... God is no respecter of persons,"** but it means the same thing: no partiality, no respecter of persons. Notice that in Verse 35, the Bible says:

> **"But in every nation whoever fears Him and works righteousness is accepted by Him."**

If I am part of the black nation, and if "every nation" includes all nations—which it must, because *every* is an all-inclusive term—then I am included. If I work righteousness and do the will, plan and purpose of God, and I am accepted by God, then who should not accept me? Peter said, **"I perceive that God shows no partiality...."** If God does not show partiality, how can we? Why should any of us show partiality, unless we are prejudiced?

In Acts 17:24-25, it says:

> **"God, who made the world and everything in it, since He is Lord of heaven and earth, does not dwell in temples made with hands.**
>
> **"Nor is He worshiped with men's hands, as though He needed anything, since He gives to all life, breath, and all things."**

Since God **"gives to all life, breath, and all things,"** that means God gives life and breath to white people, black people, red people,

---

[1] All biblical quotes are taken from the *New King James Version* unless otherwise noted.

yellow people and brown people. Consequently, it's hard to understand why one ethnic group should have the attitude that it has something special. They got theirs—**"life, breath, and all things"**—from the same place that I got mine, so how could it possibly make them better than me? And how could it possibly make me inferior to them?

Acts 17:25-26 tells us:

> **"Nor is He worshiped with men's hands, as though He needed anything, since He gives to all life, breath, and all things.**
>
> **"And He has made from one blood every nation of men to dwell on all the face of the earth, and has determined their preappointed times and the boundaries of their dwellings."**

Notice again the first part of the 26th verse:

> **"And He has made from one blood every nation of men to dwell on all the face of the earth...."**

The Bible says that there is only one blood; biologically, there is no such thing as black blood or white, red, yellow or brown blood. There is only one blood. If groups of people isolate themselves from the general population, they will inbreed and develop certain characteristics that would not have been developed in the out-group. That is why there may appear to be a difference between so-called racial groups, but it is all the same blood.[2]

A hematologist will tell you that you can give transfusions from any racial group to any other racial group with comparable blood types. It all works. Why? Because blood is blood is blood is blood. God only made one blood, not six bloods, not five bloods.

The Bible says **"... from one blood...."**

---

[2] I will discuss this in more detail in Part Two, Chapters 4-8.

So there is no such thing as inferior blood. Black blood is no more inferior than white blood, red blood, yellow blood or brown blood, because there is only one blood, just as there is only one human race.

Some white people believe they are superior, and that all darker races are inferior. But some Blacks are as white as Whites. Where do they come from? From slave masters, who created them by mixing so-called superior white blood with the so-called inferior black blood, thereby creating varying shades of black people from blue black to snow white.

I say it again: Christians ought to have the same attitude that God has toward other ethnic groups, and if we don't, then I question whether we know God.

Romans 2:10-11 says:

> **but glory, honor, and peace to everyone who works what is good, to the Jew first and also to the G eek.**
>
> **For there is no partiality with God.**

In the traditional *King James*, Verse 11 says:

> **For there is no respect of persons with God.**

God shows no partiality, so we cannot—not if we still consider ourselves Christians. We can be churchgoers; we can be religious, but how can we be born by God's Spirit and not have some of God in us? And if **...there is no partiality with God**, where do we get partiality? How can we say we know God and show partiality when He does not?

The Bible says, **"By the mouth of two or three witnesses every word shall be established"** (2 Corinthians 13:1), and I have provided three Scriptures, so I am biblically correct. But I am going to provide further witness. Second Corinthians 5:14-17 tells us:

How God Sees Humanity

> **For the love of Christ compels us, because we judge thus: that if One died for all, then all died;**
>
> **and He died for all, that those who live should live no longer for themselves, but for Him who died for them and rose again.**
>
> **Therefore, from now on, we regard no one according to the flesh. Even though we have known Christ according to the flesh, yet now we know Him thus no longer**
>
> **Therefore, if anyone is in Christ, he is a new creation; old things have passed away; behold, all things have become new.**

God says in Verse 16, **we regard no one according to the flesh...** But the Church does! Christians do, and, primarily, white Christians do.

I am not saying every white Christian does, but there are too many who do, and those who don't have not taken a stand against those who do, so they are guilty, too. Under the law, they are called accessories after the fact. They did not go into the bank, they did not pull out a gun, they did not put bandannas on their faces, but they drove the getaway car. They are as guilty as the rest. If they do not say anything against it, that means they are for it. Their silence condemns them. And this pattern of complicity started with the church leaders.

Some Blacks have developed a racist attitude toward Whites. It is a reactive racism to help Blacks keep their sanity in the face of the racist actions and attitudes black people are confronted with on a daily basis, like getting stopped and questioned by the police for driving our own cars simply because we don't have white skin—a "crime" some have dubbed DWB (Driving While Black).

But does this make Blacks' reactive racism right? No; it goes as much against the Word of God as Whites' racist attitudes toward Blacks. It goes against God's Word to let the bitterness of racism get into any of us and make us act like those who have hurt us. It is against God's Word for any of us to show prejudice—partiality—with respect to any group or individual: white, Hispanic, Asian, Native American, black or any other. For God made us all of one blood and He shows no partiality; and He told us to **... regard no one according to the flesh...**

The conflicts between light- and dark-skinned Blacks are also a result of society's racism. They were inspired by slave owners as part of their strategy to divide and conquer: If you can keep people scattered and fragmented, they can never join together, act as one and defend their rights; that way you can control them better.

Slave owners needed some slaves to work inside the houses and others to work out in the fields. The slaves that were in the field were called field niggers, while the slaves that worked inside the house were called house niggers. Comparatively, house niggers had it made. They were there with the white man; they were with the boss, with "Massa," right under Massa's nose. They cleaned Massa's house, they washed Massa's sheets, they served Massa's food, while the field niggers were picking the cotton, the corn and doing all the dirty work.

People have to survive, and they will find the way they can survive best. The house niggers did not want the field niggers to get into the house, because they were afraid of being replaced by them. The slave owners exploited that attitude to keep Blacks divided against each other, and we learned the lesson so well that even though it is against God's Word, we are still perpetuating that idiotic syndrome today.

Again, Verse 16 says:

> **Therefore, from now on, we regard no one according to the flesh...**

This means I should not evaluate any people according to their flesh, nor should they evaluate me according to my flesh or anyone else according to his or her flesh—no one, ever, at any time.

If that is the case, then any black person is good enough to marry any white person. In the days of slavery, there was never anything said about a white man sexually assaulting a black woman; that was all right—indeed, it was a common practice.[3] But even today we as a society have a problem with a black man dating or marrying a white woman or a black woman dating or marrying a white man. That we cannot tolerate.

The underlying issue of race prejudice is sexual, and nobody wants to deal with that. But if we do not get down to the cause, we cannot fix it. The problem is bigger than most people realize. Christians could stop it, but instead we are perpetuating it because we are the biggest offenders. When I say "we," I'm talking about the Church. The Church has not done what it was supposed to do.

In Galatians 2:6, Paul tells us:

> **But from those who seemed to be something—whatever they were, it makes no difference to me; God shows personal favoritism to no man—for those who seemed to be something added nothing to me.**

If God shows personal favoritism to no man, it means God does not show personal favoritism to white people, black people, red people, yellow people or brown people. So if I am His child, I can't show personal favoritism either.

---

[3] See Angela Y. Davis, *Women, Race, and Class* (New York: Vintage Books, a division of Random House, 1983), 175. Davis discusses the problematic rape of black women and the myth of the rapist that has been historically perpetuated: "Slavery relied as much on the routine sexual abuse as it relied on the whip and the lash. Excessive sex urges, whether they existed among individual white men or not, had nothing to do with this virtual institutionalization of rape. Sexual coercion was, rather, an essential dimension of the social relations between slave master and slave."

Galatians 3:28 says:

There is neither Jew nor Greek, there is neither slave nor free, there is neither male nor female; for you are all one in Christ Jesus.

If we **are all one in Christ Jesus**, then I ought to be able to marry a white person or anyone else I choose. I keep bringing marriage up because that is the thing that sticks in the white craw. I already have a wonderful wife; I have been married for more than 46 years, and I am certainly not looking for another one. The only reason I am referring to intermarriage is that it is the issue that nobody wants to bring out in the open and talk about. Who you marry—that is the real issue.

I don't care who anyone marries, but if someone does have a problem with one racial choice over another, then I have to ask why. Since God shows no partiality and God shows personal favoritism to no man—no white man, no black man, no red man, no yellow man and no brown man—why do you?

James 2:9 tells us:

but if you show partiality, you commit sin, and are convicted by the law as transgressors.

The traditional *King James* says it this way:

But if ye have respect to persons, ye commit sin....

We are used to thinking that getting drunk is a sin and using drugs is a sin and "shacking up" is a sin, and they are. But we have never considered that this morass of partiality, this morass of superiority/inferiority, is sin. We don't consider it a sin, but God does.

Let's look at 1 Peter 1:13-17:

Therefore gird up the loins of your mind, be sober, and rest your hope fully upon the grace that is to be brought to you at the revelation of Jesus Christ;

as obedient children, not conforming yourselves to the former lusts, as in your ignorance;

but as He who called you is holy, you also be holy in all your conduct,

because it is written, *"Be holy, for I am holy."*

And if you call on the Father, who without partiality judges according to each one's work, conduct yourselves throughout the time of your stay here in fear.

The last verse tells us:

And if you call on the Father, who without partiality judges according to each one's work....

How does God judge? **... Without partiality ... according to each one's work....** God judges the content of my character, not the color of my skin. So my question is, who has a right to judge me by my skin color when God does not judge this way?

If we fail to stop this in the Church, what chance does the world have?

This question was brought home to me on a gut level by a traumatic incident that happened in my life.

5
The Catalyst

To me, racism is evil because it is an affront to God. In fact, racism is telling God that He is a blithering idiot because He did not know that when He created black people, He was creating an inferior product. If you are a racist, in essence that is what you are saying.

Of course, racists are not only calling God a fool, they are also flying in the face of all logic: How could God create all men out of one blood and only the black part of those whom He created is inferior?

The Bible tells us to **abstain from every form of evil** (1 Thessalonians 5:22). Racism is evil; racial, ethnic and color prejudice are evil; they do not come from God and they are not of faith. Therefore, they are sin. We should even abstain from the appearance of racism because, as the Bible says, we should abstain from whatever looks evil. Some white people do not know this is in the Bible. Their ministers have withheld it from them to keep them in the dark that there was something wrong in the way they were brought up.

Romans 12:17 says:

Repay no one evil for evil. Have regard for good things in the sight of all men.

The traditional *King James* says it this way:

Recompense to no man evil for evil. Provide things honest in the sight of all men.

Let's focus on the word *honest*. My reading of the organized church world in America, which is basically presided over by Whites (since Whites are the majority of society), is that it has not been as honest as white supremacists such as the one whose recorded message I quoted in Chapter 3. The white-supremacist philosophy is abominable, but they are honest about their views; they leave no doubt about how they feel about black people, and I appreciate that.

Some Whites are treacherously elusive, and it is hard to know exactly where they stand. As a black man, you will get a warm smile, a handshake, an expression of friendship, but if your son goes to their house to date their daughter, you've got a problem. That is not honest. They ought to just come out and say, "We don't like niggers and we don't want any niggers in our family." Then we would know to avoid them.

In Hebrews 13:18, the *King James Version* says:

Pray for us: for we trust we have a good conscience, in all things willing to live honestly.

To live honestly means to tell me what you are thinking. Don't shake my hand and give me a charismatic hug and act as if you love me when you really see me as a nigger. Don't do that to me. Tell me the truth. If you don't like me, fine. If you don't want my children around your children, fine. But don't let our kids play together when they are babies and small children, and then suddenly, when they grow up and are attracted to each other, tell me my son can't date your daughter. Tell me from day one that you don't like black people and you don't want the possibility of black people in your family.

This emphasis on honesty is in the Bible. In 2 Corinthians 8:21 (KJV), it says:

> **Providing for honest things, not only in the sight of the Lord, but also in the sight of men.**

When it says **sight of men**, it means black men, white men, red men, yellow men and brown men. We must be honest in the view of everyone.

In 2 Corinthians 13:7 (KJV), Paul says:

> **Now I pray to God that ye do no evil; not that we should appear approved, but that ye should do that which is honest, though we be as reprobates.**

Notice, again, the word *honest*. Honest means truthful; it means speaking from your heart. It doesn't mean living one way behind closed doors and presenting another face to the public.

In Ephesians 4:25, Paul says:

> **Therefore, putting away lying....**

We not only lie by words, we lie by actions. If you smile at me but don't like me because I am black, that is lying. And Paul tells us to put away lying.

> **Therefore, putting away lying, *"Let each one of you speak truth with his neighbor,"* for we are members of one another.**

I believe in the truth, the whole truth and nothing but the truth, so help me God. I also believe that, as Paul teaches us, we are members of one another. That is why the incident I am going to tell you about was so traumatic to me, so traumatic that it catalyzed me to take up my assignment from God and take on the subject of racism and religion. The incident is an example both of apparent racism and of apparent dishonesty. What made it particularly painful was that it occurred with someone I thought of as a friend; what made it particularly significant was that the man was a minister.

The incident began for me when a group of black ministers gave me a tape of a Sunday-morning sermon delivered in 1992 by a prominent white charismatic minister whom I knew well. My fellow black ministers were disturbed by the sermon, which was heard by thousands of people worldwide. In presenting the sermon here, it is not my purpose to malign the white minister in any way, but rather to identify an apparent racial problem. I have deleted all names mentioned on the tape, because I am not interested in naming names. I am interested only in the content of what is being said, because I think that it speaks to the subject of racism and that it is symptomatic of the problem and shows where the issues lie. Please read the following transcription with an open mind and with an open heart:

> ... I can't tell your kids who to go with and who not to go date. Not my responsibility. If you don't want your kids dating somebody, then you control it. But you control it a long time before they ever get to be dating age. You talk about we're friends. We can be friends with everybody; we are not prejudiced, but we are not going to date this group of people; it's not in our culture to do it. We're not going to do it. If you want to, there's no problem with that; that's fine. You're not a racist, and you're not prejudiced just because you set down those kinds of rules. Hello?
>
> If you want, if you want, if you want mixed, fine. That's if you want it, that's fine! But if you don't want it, then you control it. And you don't have to be a racist about it. And I'm not afraid to talk about it because I've got thirty percent of a different, of black, in this congregation. And I've talked to many of them, talked to the men about it; I've talked to a lot of these people about it, and they all understand where I'm coming from. We got some beautiful mixed marriages in our congregation, but I have talked to them also and they have not been without their problems.

Hello? Come on people, let's be, let's get our head out of the sand. And I'll get accused again, like I always do, that I'm against mixed marriages. I did not say I was against mixed marriages. I said it's up to you. But if you don't want your kids involved in it, then you're the one that has to do something about it, not the church. And just because you change churches, it's not going to help the problem. Some people say, "Well, we'll change churches." No. "We'll move away; we'll go somewhere else and start all over." No, it's not—You're just going to take the problem with you. Hello?

Many years ago, [my daughter] was in the kindergarten. We came home, and this young little man was there, nice young man, and we just talked to [my daughter]. We said, "Hey, look, we're friends, we play, we go together as groups, but we don't date one another." I mean, we started in kindergarten. Hello? That just was our rule. Now once somebody gets up and they get of age—they get to be twenty-one, eighteen—then they can choose to do what they want to; you ain't got no choice. You, you can't do [anything] about it; they're on their own. I'll tell you what. The Bible says if you train a child up the way you want it to go, when it gets old, it won't depart. It may wobble around a while, but it'll come back. Hello?

You say, "Well, my Lord and soul, Pastor, you [are] talking heavy." I am and I've gotten close to the air conditioner 'cause I'm sweating like everything. But I'll tell you something. I just decided that if I'm going to teach on it, I'm going to turn over every stone there is! Like it or lump it, amen or oh me.

Now, I'm going to tell you what. I'm white and I'm saying this so a lot of people say, "Yeah, he's white." Hey, we have had a lot of the, the black parents that have come to us and have said, "We don't like this, we don't want this, how do we stop it?" Hello? The same way we do. Hello? That we enjoy fellowship with one another, that

> we can go together as groups, we can live and work together—we just don't go with one another, and we just don't mix our races. There's only thirteen percent of the population that is of your color. If we continue to mix it, [there] ain't going to be none of you left. There ain't nobody going to be able to say, "Black is beautiful"; they're going to have to say, "Mixed is beautiful."
>
> I don't mean that wrong. I don't think that we ought to mix any of the races. That's my personal opinion, okay? I'm not, I didn't tell you not to do it, and I'm not going to throw you out if you have, but I'm talking about an issue that we have a problem with.
>
> My wife said quit. It is a problem that is being had all over the United States, not just here. But if we will establish relationships, we can have tremendous results. And we can live and work together in unity and harmony and we can be what God wants us to be. We can live right, talk right, do what God wants. But parents, don't provoke your children. Children, don't provoke your parents. Obey them if you want to live long, and I've gone too long. I'm sorry, bow your heads, please.

I was as disturbed by the tape as my colleagues were. The recorded version of this excerpt was eight minutes long. A man does not say what this man said off the cuff over an eight-minute period; there's a biblical principle that says that out of the abundance of the heart the mouth speaks (Matthew 12:34). What was in the heart of the minister who delivered this sermon? And why was it there?

I am going to review sections of the transcript in order to comment on them, beginning with one that I feel is central to the problem:

> I can't tell your kids who to go with and who not to go date. Not my responsibility. If you don't want your kids dating somebody, then you control it. But you control it a long time before they ever get to be dating age.

This is where racism comes from. As I mentioned before, we who are alive today, black and white, did not start racism. We are all the result of how we have been brought up. Certain attitudes were planted in our minds when we were children, some directly and some subliminally. And when we see certain things, they generate a response, like Pavlov's dog; if you ring a bell, the dog salivates, even when there is nothing to salivate about. The dog has been conditioned to salivate when he hears the bell, whether he sees food or not. Some people react negatively when they see a black face. They react negatively because they have been conditioned to react negatively—and this conditioning started in the home.

This minister is instructing his congregation to teach their children before the children reach dating age. Many white people, especially southern Whites, have trained their children this way. Racism is not in the genes, it starts in the home. I am not saying every white person is a racist. When Adolf Hitler came to power, it did not take every person who was a German citizen to slaughter millions of innocent people. So it doesn't have to be everybody. It can be just enough to start a war and extinguish the lives of the millions of Jewish people and other people the Nazis found undesirable.

> You talk about we're friends. We can be friends with everybody; we are not prejudiced, but we are not going to date this group of people; it's not in our culture to do it. We're not going to do it.

If you do not want to date certain people, that's fine with me. But there is a law of cause and effect that says for every effect, there is a cause. If the effect is, "... we are not going to date this group of people," there must be a cause. I want to know what that cause is. Why don't you date these people? The Scriptures tell us to be honest. If you are honest, you have to tell me, why not date this group of people? God does not have a problem with it, so why do you?

> If you want to, there's no problem with that; that's fine. You're not a racist, and you're not prejudiced

> just because you set down those kinds of rules. Hello?
>
> If you want, if you want, if you want mixed, fine. That's if you want it, that's fine! But if you don't want it, then you control it. And you don't have to be a racist about it. And I'm not afraid to talk about it because I've got thirty percent of a different, of black, in this congregation.

Once more we see that it is an issue of Blacks and Whites. The minister doesn't refer to Hispanics or Asians in his congregation, why does he refer only to the Blacks?

I am dealing with a symptom here, not the man. But he represents something. When you are a leader and you stand in the pulpit and minister to people, people are going to believe that what you say is from God. That is how racism in America became the mess it is today, because of so-called leaders and ministers talking in this way. Nobody has challenged them.

That day is over.

Let's look at what the minister says about mixed marriages:

> I've talked to a lot of these people about it, and they all understand where I'm coming from. We got some beautiful mixed marriages in our congregation, but I have talked to them also and they have not been without their problems.

In essence, he is saying that only mixed marriages have marital problems. So if you stay within your own ethnicity and only marry people of your kind, you are not going to have any marital problems.

A marital problem is a marital problem. I don't care if it is a financial problem, a child-discipline problem, a temper problem, a sexual problem, a wife-beating problem, a husband-beating problem, a molesting-of-kids problem, a drug problem, an alcohol problem. Whatever it is, it is still a problem and it can wreck a marriage. I don't know of any married couple that at some time has not had some kind of problem.

> Hello? Come on people, let's be, let's get our head out of the sand. And I'll get accused again, like I always do, that I'm against mixed marriages. I did not say I was against mixed marriages.

This is where it becomes truly mind-boggling. He says, "I am not against mixed marriages"; if that is the case, he should have nothing else to say about it, because if he is not against something, he is either for it or, at the very least, neutral about it.

> I said it's up to you. But if you don't want your kids involved in it, then you're the one that has to do something about it, not the church.

Not the Church? If the Church does not have an influence on how you live your life and raise your kids, what on God's green earth are the Church and the Bible good for? If the Church and the Bible are not going to have any influence on people's actions and thoughts, then what is?

> And just because you change churches, it's not going to help the problem. Some people say, "Well, we'll change churches." No. "We'll move away; we'll go somewhere else and start all over." No, it's not—You're just going to take the problem with you. Hello?

Why is it a problem? God never says it is a problem. Why is it a problem? It is only a problem when you object to it, but just because you object to it does not make it wrong.

> Many years ago, [my daughter] was in the kindergarten....

That is where racist conditioning starts; a little child's impressionable mind is like a piece of raw clay—it can be easily molded.

> We came home, and this young little man was there, nice young man, and we just talked to [my daughter]. We

> said, "Hey, look, we're friends, we play, we go together as groups, but we don't date one another." I mean, we started in kindergarten. Hello?

Imagine what kind of message this sent to that innocent child? Obviously, from that point forward, she is going to think that there is something wrong with *those* people. That is how it starts: subliminally. And every time a child who has been raised this way sees one of *those* people, his or her subliminal programming sends a message that there must be something wrong with *that* race.

> That just was our rule. Now once somebody gets up and they get of age—they get to be twenty-one, eighteen—then they can choose to do what they want to; you ain't got no choice. You, you can't do [anything] about it; they're on their own. I'll tell you what. The Bible says if you train a child up the way you want it to go, when it gets old, it won't depart.

This man was raised on the Bible. He did not just get saved three weeks before he preached that sermon. He has been around the Word of God since before he was born. It is almost in his genes, so to speak. So what he was saying here was not a mistake.

Notice that he is telling his congregation that the Bible says, "You train a child up the way you want it to go...." The Bible does not say that. The Bible says, **Train up a child in the way he should go, and when he is old he will not depart from it** (Proverbs 22:6). You train a child in the way he *should* go, which is God's way, not in your own racist, prejudiced way. If everyone trained his or her children in the ways of God, there would be no racism. The problem occurs because parents are racists and they pass the disease on to their children.

> You say, "Well my Lord and soul, Pastor, you [are] talking heavy." I am and I've gotten close to the air conditioner 'cause I'm sweating like everything. But I'll tell you something. I just decided that if I'm going to teach on it, I'm

> going to turn over every stone there is! Like it or lump it, amen or oh me.

This is where we find out that nothing the man has to say on this subject is offhand. He tells us that he "decided" that if he was "going to teach on it" he was "going to turn over every stone there is." Therefore, his statements were *decided* on; they were premeditated.

> Now, I'm going to tell you what. I'm white and I'm saying this so a lot of people say, "Yeah, he's white." Hey, we have had a lot of the, the black parents that have come to us and have said, "We don't like this, we don't want this, how do we stop it?" Hello? The same way we do. Hello? That we enjoy fellowship with one another, that we can go together as groups, we can live and work together—we just don't go with one another, and we just don't mix our races. There's only thirteen percent of the population that is of your color. If we continue to mix it, [there] ain't going to be none of you left. There ain't nobody going to be able to say, "Black is beautiful"; they're going to have to say, "Mixed is beautiful."

What is wrong with mixed, if you want it? What is bad about mixed? The minister has an answer to that, and the answer is his personal opinion:

> I don't think that we ought to mix any of the races. That's my personal opinion, okay?

How can anyone be a minister of the Gospel, and supposedly be ministering life to people, and have an opinion that goes contrary to the Bible, and then have the audacity to express it publicly? He does not think we ought to mix any of the races. Poor old God did not know that! Why not? Out of one blood, the Scriptures tell us, God made all men to dwell on the face of the whole earth. So what is this minister's problem?

> ... I didn't tell you not to do it, and I'm not going to throw you out if you have....

If you have a mixed marriage, he will not throw you out of his congregation, but he will make you feel guilty—because he is your pastor and he does not think we ought to mix races. What kind of message is he sending to people?

> ... but I'm talking about an issue that we have a problem with....
>
> My wife said quit. It is a problem that is being had all over the United States, not just here.

He is now saying that there is a problem, but it is not the problem of racism. It is an intermarriage problem; it is mixing the inferior black blood with the superior white blood—that is the real issue.

"My wife said quit," he tells us. My question is, if he had been talking about fornication, would she have told him to quit? If he had been talking about adultery, would she have told him to quit? If he had been talking about child beating and child abuse, would she have told him to quit? If he had been talking about abortion, would she have told him to quit? He has just said that we have a problem all over America and yet his wife is telling him to stop talking about the problem. Why?

The real reason I think is that he is letting the cat out of the bag. From now on, everyone will know where he and those around him stand. They kept it a secret until now, but now it is out in the open. The man's wife was trying to tell him, "Stop! Don't talk anymore, because if you keep talking, then everybody is going to know how we truly feel on the inside." To me, that is downright dishonest.

Yes, I am angry. I am mad as the hell prepared for those who reject Jesus as Savior and Lord! I am angry, just as Jesus was angry when He went into the temple and threw out the moneychangers for selling in God's house. I am angry, just as Jesus was when He stood before the Pharisees in the presence of a man who had a withered hand. The Bible says that Jesus told the man to stand forth, and then He looked around upon the Pharisees with anger, being grieved at the hardness of their hearts, because they did not want Him to heal the man's withered hand on the Sabbath day.

I am not angry with any individual person, but I am angry about a situation that until now, apparently, nobody has fully addressed. If someone had done it 20, 50, 100 or 200 years ago, I would not be dealing with it now. That is the kind of anger I have; it is holy, righteous indignation. Do not take it personally. I am angry about a principle that should have been dealt with but was not.

> But if we will establish relationships...

How can we establish a relationship based on dishonesty? How are we going to have a relationship if you don't like me just because I am black? How are we going to have a relationship if every time I am around you and bring my son, I am on pins and needles because you are wondering whether my son is going to run off with your white daughter and marry her? How are we going to have a relationship if I am on pins and needles all the time because you are wondering whether he is going to have eyes for her or she will have eyes for him?

> ... we can have tremendous results. And we can live and work together in unity and harmony and we can be what God wants us to be. We can live right, talk right, do what God wants. But parents, don't provoke your children. Children, don't provoke your parents. Obey them if you want to live long, and I've gone too long. I'm sorry, bow your heads, please.

Again, my purpose in exposing this is not to indict the individual, but to look at and analyze the information contained in the message. To me, it *appears* to be racist. And the Bible says to abstain from every appearance of evil.

6

Why I Had to Speak Out

The delegation of black ministers who gave me the tape of the sermon were hurt, outraged and bewildered by it. They were doubly mystified that it came from a ministry that is held in such high esteem in the charismatic community. They came to me because of my longstanding relationship with that ministry.

I could have kept quiet about it; I could have just let it pass by without comment, because, at that time, I was, in essence, the house nigger of that ministry. This was not something I sought; God raised me up. I have never looked for anyone's approval; I don't need it. I'm not impressed by "big people." God is bigger than everybody, and I am with God, and that is good enough for me.

God created a relationship between this ministry and me. I did not know why at the time, but I know now. It gave those people an opportunity over a twenty-year period to see that we are just like they are. The only difference is the color of our skin. They have been in our home, they have slept in our beds and eaten at our table, so they know there really is no difference.

On hearing the taped sermon, I knew I had to respond to it. And because I responded, the situation put me back in the field. I am a field nigger now, and some others who used to be field niggers ran to the house and left me out in the field.

My writing about this is probably uncomfortable for some people, both black and white. In fact, I know that some black people will say, "Fred Price, why don't you shut your mouth? We have the opportunity to ride in the front of the bus. If you keep talking about this, they are going to put us in the back of the bus again. We've never had it as good as we have it now. Why in the world don't you leave this alone?"

My answer is that I have an assignment from God and I have to deal with it. I do not really like it; I wish it had been dealt with before I got here, but I am committed to do the job God assigned me. Some black people fear that taking a stand will make us lose the progress we've made; they are worried that racism will go from covert to overt again.

I would like black people to reflect on this: You may think things are really good now because you're riding in the front of the bus, but if white supremacists pressured the United States Congress to enact a law to deport all black people and send us back to Africa, how many of your white friends would be willing to go back to Africa with you? And how many black people do you think would stay here while the rest of us were on the boat going to Africa?

We black people need to learn how to stand together—not against anyone, but once and for all in our lives to stand for us. There is nothing wrong with that; you ought to support your own team. You are a poor player if you are not for your team. If you are on my team but are rooting for the other team to win, I don't need you on my team. Yet by and large we Blacks have been so intimidated by Whites that we have often supported the white team instead of each other—and this has become so ingrained that sometimes we do not even realize it.

The reasons for this are not hard to find. They have to do with America's whole attitude toward black culture, an attitude that is almost 400 years old, having its roots in America's "peculiar institution" of slavery.[1]

In Los Angeles, on Olympic Boulevard, there is a neighborhood in which all you see are signs in Korean. There was a time when there were hardly any Koreans in Los Angeles; now Koreans have their own stores, restaurants and businesses. Not only that, they have retained their own language: In Koreatown, you can't even read the signs in store windows if you don't know the language. Farther downtown, there is another neighborhood called Chinatown, which looks as if it might be part of China. It is filled with pagodas, Chinese lions, dragons, various trappings of Chinese culture as well as Chinese restaurants. Both communities are distinguished from the rest of the city by their unique styles, colors and alphabets.

But black people do not have a Lagostown or a Kenyatown in Los Angeles or anywhere in America. The reason for this is that historically we have not had the impulse to create one, because of the circumstances in which black people were brought here and the way we were treated. White people need to understand that since the beginning of this country's history, black people have been conditioned by being deliberately stripped of our original culture. The purpose was to make slaves completely dependent upon slave masters. Families were cold-bloodedly separated—husbands and wives torn apart, children sold from under their parents' noses, never to be

---

[1] See Robin Blackburn, *The Making of New World Slavery: From the Baroque to the Modern 1492-1800* (New York: Verso, 1997), 14. Referring to the peculiarity of slavery in America (also known as the "peculiar institution"), Blackburn states, "New World slavery was peculiarly associated with darker pigmentation or 'black' skin. Not every Black was a slave, but most Blacks were, and on this assumption every Black could be treated like a slave unless they could prove free status—and even then, they would still be treated worse than the white colonists."

seen again. How could people do this to other people? Because black people were not considered people, they were considered animals, and animals don't count. That was the concept of slavery—and the concept is a concept of inferiority.

This nation has been built on the assumption that black people are inferior and white people are superior; that is the assumption, and if you are black, you might as well face it. From the moment Blacks were abducted in Africa and brought here, everything that has been done to black people has been based on that assumption, and the effect on Blacks as a group has been devastating.

Based on his statements, I believe the minister whom I have quoted is representative of the many people who believe in the assumption of black inferiority. That is why I, as a black person, acting on biblical principles, had to withdraw fellowship. I hated having to do it, but principle means more to me than friendship. I was forced to withdraw, not out of anger at the man himself, but out of anger at a situation that after almost four centuries most people still do not want to deal with.

Today, black people in America are really white people with black skin. Why? Because Blacks don't really know how to be anything else. We don't know anything about our African culture. We don't know anything about our past. The only thing we know is the culture we were placed into.[2] Since our forefathers were inculcated with white values and passed these values down from generation to generation, Blacks have values that are very white oriented.

---

2 For centuries the history of African Americans was never taught in the United States at any educational level. Eventually, through acts of protest, students forced implementation of African-American Studies curricula at the university level in the late 1960s. In the early 1970s, several universities began to offer African-American/Black Studies as a major. See Janice E. Hale-Benson, *Black Children: Their Roots, Culture, and Learning Styles* (Baltimore: Johns Hopkins University Press, 1986), 178.

The African culture we would have needed to create a Kenyatown or a Lagostown was taken away from our ancestors when their culture and humanity were taken away in order to make them better slaves; succeeding generations, not having the African culture to remember and build on, were increasingly turned into black-skinned white Americans.[3] Whatever prejudice Asians experienced in our country's history—and there has been a great deal of it—they have retained their own culture. It might be said that losing our own culture has even reinforced the concept that Blacks are inferior, be-cause if you do not actually know the facts behind the loss, there's a subliminal impression that perhaps the culture from Africa was not worth remembering or preserving.[4]

---

3 In the past, even when Blacks emulated white society and built thriving black towns and communities based on white American models, the communities have often been destroyed by white violence. One example of this is the Black Wall Street in Tulsa, Oklahoma. A 36-block district that housed over 600 black-owned and black-operated businesses at the turn of the century, the Black Wall Street was burned to the ground on May 31, 1921, when airplanes dropped bombs on the community and an angry white mob began to annihilate it. Whites justified this attack by claiming that a black man, Dick Rowland, allegedly attacked a young white woman in an elevator, a charge that she later refused to testify to in court. See Scott Ellsworth and John Hope Franklin, *Death in a Promised Land: The Tulsa Race Riot of 1921* (Baton Rouge: Louisiana State University Press, 1982). The destruction of Tulsa's Black Wall Street was only one such tragedy in what became known as the Red Summer, because of the bloodshed in black communities across America. Cedric J. Robinson, professor of Black Studies and Political Science at University of California, Santa Barbara, reports that during that summer there were 24 other "white racist pogroms" in black neighborhoods in cities including Chicago and Washington, D.C. See Cedric J. Robinson, *Black Movements in America* (New York: Routledge, 1997), 116-117.

4 This has an extremely negative effect on black people's self-image. Professor Hale-Benson, an associate professor of early childhood

Because Blacks have been put down for so long, often they cannot accept another black person in a position of authority until white people accept him first. An instance of this is that when I was first called by God to deal with the message of faith, not one black person in America, not one black church, not one black ministry would invite me to come. God knew that black people would not receive another black man until white people had validated his authenticity, and for quite a few years, my ministry was to white people. I went to Australia four or five times. There was no one down there except white people and Aborigines, and I did not get sent to the Aborigines.

Once I got credibility among white people—and thank God for the good white people who saw the value in what God had deposited in me or I would not have had any kind of credibility or opportunity—I began to have more diverse speaking engagements. God promoted me past white people, black people, red people, yellow people and brown people. No one in America can claim the FaithDome—the largest sanctuary in America—and its ministry of 18,000 but God Almighty. And that is the reason why God gave me this assignment—because I don't owe anything to anyone except to Him.

I don't have to hold my tongue because I am not dependent on any person. I will not accept the false assumption that Blacks are inferior; I will not allow the centuries of obliteration of black culture to obliterate my identity as a black man, nor will I allow fear to keep me from standing up for my own team.

---

education at Cleveland State University, points to a related experience among black preschool children who are placed in a totally Caucasian preschool environment. Hale-Benson quotes Hakim Rashid as saying that "the African-American child who only sees the Euro-American tradition manifested in the preschool environment can only conclude that the absence of visual representations of his culture connotes his essential worthlessness." See Hale-Benson, 196.

Why I Had to Speak Out

I confronted the unnamed minister about this sermon personally, one-to-one. I am writing about it now publicly only because I believe that the principle is so important that it needs to be put on the table and dealt with in a public manner. Clandestine conversations about this subject are no longer possible. I know it is uncomfortable; I know many black people wish that I would remain silent. But I did not get my marching orders from them. I am sorry that they have become so white that they cannot see that we are black.

I have even had people tell me that others in the black community have said to them that I am "too black." How can I be too black? I am as black as God made me.

In Galatians 2:11-14, Paul says:

> **Now when Peter had come to Antioch, I withstood him to his face, because he was to be blamed;**
>
> **for before certain men came from James, he would eat with the Gentiles; but when they came, he withdrew and separated himself, fearing those who were of the circumcision.**
>
> **And the rest of the Jews also played the hypocrite with him, so that even Barnabas was carried away with their hypocrisy.**
>
> **But when I saw that they were not straightforward about the truth of the gospel, I said to Peter before them all, "If you, being a Jew, live in the manner of Gentiles and not as the Jews, why do you compel Gentiles to live as Jews?"**

Peter was a devout Jew, and he was prejudiced against the Gentiles. He would eat with the Gentiles when the Jews were not present, but when the Jews came in, he would go over and eat with the Jews, and would not eat with the Gentiles. Paul called him on the carpet.

That is all I am doing. God gave me this assignment to do publicly. I repeat, I don't like it, but I would like it less to be standing before the Judgment Seat of Almighty God and the Lord Jesus Christ and having Him point His finger at me and say, "Fred, I gave you an assignment. Why didn't you fulfill it?"

Man is not going to reward me, so I cannot afford to be concerned about what men think. I am only concerned about what God will say to me when I stand before His throne.

Not everyone is going to understand where I am coming from, but if someone does not understand the message, then it is not for him anyway; it is only for those who have ears to hear and eyes to see. There is a segment of people who are ready to hear, and God knows that. He has to have a spokesman; He does not talk out of heaven, He talks through the ministry gifts that He sets in the Church, but He can only speak to the degree that the vessels are willing to allow Him to speak.

Matthew 25:31-46 says:

> **"When the Son of Man comes in His glory, and all the holy angels with Him, then He will sit on the throne of His glory.**
>
> **"All the nations will be gathered before Him, and He will separate them one from another, as a shepherd divides his sheep from the goats.**
>
> **"And He will set the sheep on His right hand, but the goats on the left.**
>
> **"Then the King will say to those on His right hand, 'Come, you blessed of My Father, inherit the kingdom prepared for you from the foundation of the world:**
>
> **'for I was hungry and you gave Me food; I was thirsty and you gave Me drink; I was a stranger and you took Me in;**

'I was naked and you clothed Me; I was sick and you visited Me; I was in prison and you came to Me.'

"Then the righteous will answer Him, saying, 'Lord, when did we see You hungry and feed You, or thirsty and give You drink?

'When did we see You a stranger and take You in, or naked and clothe You?

'Or when did we see You sick, or in prison, and come to You?'

"And the King will answer and say to them, 'Assuredly, I say to you, inasmuch as you did it to one of the least of these My brethren, you did it to Me.'

"Then He will also say to those on the left hand, 'Depart from Me, you cursed, into the everlasting fi e prepared for the devil and his angels:

'for I was hungry and you gave Me no food; I was thirsty and you gave Me no drink;

'I was a stranger and you did not take Me in, naked and you did not clothe Me, sick and in prison and you did not visit Me.'

"Then they also will answer Him, saying, 'Lord, when did we see You hungry or thirsty or a stranger or naked or sick or in prison, and did not minister to You?'

"Then He will answer them, saying, 'Assuredly, I say to you, inasmuch as you did not do it to one of the least of these, you did not do it to Me.'

"And these will go away into everlasting punishment, but the righteous into eternal life."

I am black. I did not make myself this way; I was born this way. And I will always be black. And so I stand with those who are black.

My withdrawal from the minister was based on this premise: If the ministry that produced this message has any reservations about any black person, it has reservations about me. I cannot be comfortable being your friend if you have a funny attitude about those who are of my color. I will not accept that. I hate that our relationship had to be ruptured, but I have to stand with those who are my color.

Jesus said, inasmuch as you have done it to the least of these, you have done it to Me; and since you did not do it to the least of these, you did not do it to Me. Jesus takes people's actions personally; He counts them as though they were done to Him, and that is the way I feel. If you do not accept my brother, you do not accept me. That is the way it is.

Let's look at another example to illustrate my point. In Acts 9, the Apostle Paul is on the Damascus road. Paul was not a Christian at the time, and he was threatening the Church. He had obtained letters from the high priest to take those who called on the name of Jesus and put them in prison. He even stood by and consented to those people being killed.

Acts 9:1-5 tells us:

> **Then Saul** [Paul]**, still breathing threats and murder against the disciples of the Lord, went to the high priest**
>
> **and asked letters from him to the synagogues of Damascus, so that if he found any who were of the Way, whether men or women, he might bring them bound to Jerusalem.**
>
> **As he journeyed he came near Damascus, and suddenly a light shone around him from heaven.**
>
> **Then he fell to the ground, and heard a voice saying to him, "Saul, Saul, why are you persecuting Me?"**

Why I Had to Speak Out

> **And he said, "Who are You, Lord?" Then the Lord said, "I am Jesus, whom you are persecuting. It is hard for you to kick against the goads."**

Consider this: Paul the Apostle never saw Jesus physically, never walked with Jesus physically, never put his hand on Jesus physically, never put Jesus in prison physically, never had any kind of contact with Jesus physically, yet Jesus takes what Paul did very personally. He said, "...why are you persecuting me?" Why did Jesus say this? Because His Church is Him. Jesus takes what is done against the Church very personally, and so I take what is done against my black brethren just as personally.

If you do not like my brothers and sisters because they are black, you do not like me. I'm not going to let you praise me and tell me how nice I am if you do not also consider my brothers and sisters praiseworthy and nice, even though they, too, are black. I don't need that kind of acceptance. When the boats let down the gangplanks at the pier and we black people are boarded onto those boats to head back to Africa, is it likely that I'm going to be the only black person standing on the pier watching them go? They are going to send me, too.

I'm attempting to explain precisely why I felt it necessary to withdraw. The following Scriptures are not a perfect exegesis of the Greek, but there is a principle that I would like to extract. I am bringing this up because I don't want a theologian reading this to accuse me of incorrect exegesis of the text; I am focusing on a principle, and I believe it is valid.

Romans 16:17 says:

> **Now I urge you, brethren, note those who cause divisions and offenses....**

I was offended by that tape; I was offended by the minister telling everybody in the world that something is wrong with me, just because I am black, just because of the color of my skin.

> ... We can be friends ... but we are not going to date this group of people. It's not in our culture to do it. We're not going to do it.

That is an offensive statement. Note that in this Scripture, it is God talking:

> **Now I urge you, brethren, note those who cause divisions and offenses, contrary to the doctrine which you learned, and avoid them.**

I had to withdraw because the message was offensive. If it was offensive to one of my brothers, or to one of my sisters, it was offensive to me. I have to avoid those who give offense, because that is what God tells all of us to do.

In 2 Thessalonians 3, there is another principle that I would like to extract. Verse 6 says:

> **But we command you, brethren, in the name of our Lord Jesus Christ, that you withdraw from every brother who walks disorderly and not according to the tradition which he received from us.**

And so I had to withdraw. Verses 10 through 14 of that same chapter tell us:

> **For even when we were with you, we commanded you this: If anyone will not work, neither shall he eat.**
>
> **For we hear that there are some who walk among you in a disorderly manner, not working at all, but are busybodies.**
>
> **Now those who are such we command and exhort through our Lord Jesus Christ that they work in quietness and eat their own bread.**
>
> **But as for you, brethren, do not grow weary in doing good.**

Why I Had to Speak Out

And if anyone does not obey our word in this epistle, note that person and do not keep company with him, that he may be ashamed.

That was my purpose for withdrawing. I had to break fellowship so that, hopefully, the minister who had given offense, and those who supported him, would be ashamed and repent of it. If you just keep saying, "I'm not an alcoholic; I'm not, I don't have a drinking problem, hic, hic. I can hold my liquor. I'm not drunk, after all; I mean, I drive better when I've had a few drinks," you will never get any help. The first step to deliverance—from alcohol or anything—is to admit, "I've got a problem; I need some help." As long as you keep denying it, you will never be free. The same first step was needed here: The minister needed to face the situation honestly and see if he had a problem; if he did, he needed to admit it so that he could then be delivered from it.

I did not withdraw from fellowship right away. I felt I wanted to see the man in person to have a conversation with him about it, and since he lived several hundred miles away, I had to wait until we were both in the same geographical place.

Six months after I heard the tape, he came to Los Angeles. Betty and I had an opportunity to be with him and his wife. In fact, I had the opportunity to drive them to the airport to catch their flight back to their state. While we were in the car, I played the tape and asked him why he had said what he did. He and his wife were upset, and for a while he couldn't even complete a sentence. Finally, he told me that he viewed Betty and me differently, that he had never looked on us that way.

For me, this response comes under the classification of house nigger and field nigger, and I am not going to be a house nigger while my people are in the field; if we are not all accepted in the house equally and as equals, I do not want to be in the house at all.

The minister assured me, with tears in his eyes, that he was not a racist. He also assured me he had never taught his daughter racist values. I told him that if he did not really mean the things that he had said, there was a simple way to rectify the situation: Just stand at the podium again and, from his heart, recant in public the statements he had made on the tape.

When Betty and I let him and his wife off in front of the airline terminal, I looked forward to his recantation so that we could put this breach behind us.

7

The Minister's Response

Once the minister returned home, I waited and waited for his statement. Remember, I had called for a retraction, not an apology. For me, apologizing was not the issue: Either he taught his daughter not to date Blacks or he didn't; either he does not care who marries whom or he does care. These were the issues that needed to be addressed publicly. Finally, he sent me a tape of his statement.

> Before I minister this morning, I want one last time to read a statement; some of you might say, well, what's it about? Well, if you're in that category, just forget it; don't even try to find out, all right? It's not worth it, worth it. Right? The last of February and in March, I did a series of messages on the home and family called *The Church at Your House*. I have apologized for this before, but one last time, I will make an attempt. In one of the lessons I made a few statements that came out all wrong; I wish to apologize for those statements and ask for forgiveness for them. All I can say is that I'm sorry for them and ask your understanding for the unfounded and uncalled-for statements.

> ... You may ask, why have you made this statement? Today, I made this statement because of the tape that is being circulated and it has caused so much hurt, and therefore, I have made the statement in the effort to clear the hurt and confusion. I thank you. God bless you.

To say that I was gravely disappointed with this message does not begin to describe how disappointed I was. The minister recanted nothing; he did not even mention the issue of racism; he merely apologized—without even referring to what he was apologizing for. It seemed as if he just wanted to get the whole thing over with as soon as possible.

In desperation, I wrote to the leader of the ministry, who is this man's father. In my seven-page letter, I laid out all the points I felt were pertinent to the matter. I received no satisfactory response. After awhile, I wrote again, summarizing everything. I am going to share part of my letter with you in order to discuss the enormity of the principles involved.

But first, think about this: I am a minister of the Gospel; I represent God to people. I cannot lie to you and get away with it. God is not going to let me do that. I am wrong if I do that. If I want to lie to myself, that's fine, but I have no right to lie to the people for whom Christ died. And if I do lie to them, I need to be man enough to come back before them and say, "You know what? I blew it. I lied. I've asked God to forgive me and I've repented of it."

Ministers need to be called into question. If they are not right, they need to be called on to give an account of their stewardship. This includes me as well as every other minister.

The ministry I am discussing is a father-and-son ministry. Before I present my letter, I want to talk about fathers and sons in the ministry, and I want to use my own son as an illustration. My son has acknowledged the call to the ministry. As the pastor of Crenshaw Christian Center, if I have him preach a sermon, and in the context of his sermon he says, "I don't believe that Blacks should marry

Blacks, I believe Blacks should marry non-Blacks," some people in the congregation would be shocked.

Since I am the pastor of the church and it would be my son who made the statement—a statement that cannot be substantiated or supported by the Scripture—and I've never said anything about the subject publicly myself, what conclusion would my congregation draw about what he said? It seems to me that my congregation would think that I must agree with him; perhaps they would even think that I taught it to him.

This is what makes it an enormous issue to me, and it is why I asked the father as well as the son to address it, and why I am writing about it. We always have to be aware of how things appear. That is why in 1 Thessalonians 5:22 (KJV), the Bible tells us to **abstain from all appearance of evil**. Things may appear to be one way when they are not, and therefore we must correct the appearance of evil.

Between my first letter to the leader of the ministry and my second, I did everything I could to get a response that would correct the situation. I talked on the telephone, I sent videotapes and audiotapes of meetings in which people from our church gave their impressions of what they heard on the tape. My objective was to get across to the ministry how crucial this issue was. Still there was no willingness to deal with the issue; it was like talking to a wall. That was when I decided to write one last time to the head of the ministry. Here is part of my letter:

> I appreciate that neither you nor [your son, who delivered the original message] believe that one race is inferior or superior to another. However, the perception by many is that in your eyes, one race is inferior or superior to the other. This perception is borne out of the statements below, which were taken verbatim from [his] original message. What you may not be aware of is that [for racists] different races do not mix, or date, or intermarry because one is believed to be inferior or

> superior. The supposition is that if they mix, they might date; and if they date, they might marry; and since the genes are inferior or superior, this would pose a problem during procreation. [His] statements, as you will see, so closely resembled these beliefs, that this is why I was so concerned and felt so strongly that if he clearly did not, in fact, believe this, once I called it to his attention, that he could in the same context make an unqualified statement to that effect.

I had already explained to the man that my congregation had heard the tape and that we had a consensus of opinion: The majority of people indicated they had gotten the impression that the speaker was racist; that was the *appearance.*

What I was asking for was the correction of that appearance: If the appearance of evil was presented by verbal communication in a public forum, the way to reverse the situation was to recant in the same public forum. If the head of the ministry and his son actually did not hold racist beliefs—if they recognized that having these beliefs was a sin—it seemed to me a simple matter for the son to go back into the same public forum and admit, from his heart, that he had been grievously wrong in what he had said. If he were to recant, then the people who had gotten the tape of the first message would be able to get the tape of the second, and therein would be the restitution.

My letter continues:

> ... This is why I was so concerned and felt so strongly that if he clearly did not, in fact, believe this, once I called it to his attention, that he could in the same context make an unqualified statement to that effect.
>
> [He] made the following statements:
>
> "We can be friends with everybody; we are not prejudiced, but we are not going to date this group of people. It's not in our culture to do it."

> We just wanted him to say he didn't care about whom his children dated.

I could not understand why if the son did not care whom his children dated, he refused to say so publicly. The only reason I could think of was that it wasn't in the man's heart to say it; that what he had said the first time was in his heart. Under the law this is called circumstantial evidence, and it can be very damaging.

In that original message, the son said:

> Many years ago, [my daughter] was in the kindergarten. We came home, and this young little man was there, nice young man, and we just talked to [my daughter]. We said, "Hey, look, we're friends, we play, we go together as groups, but we don't date one another." I mean, we started in kindergarten. Hello? That just was our rule.

As I mentioned, when I took the man and his wife to the airport, played the tape and called him on it, he told me in front of his wife and my wife that they did not teach their daughter that. I have good hearing and an excellent memory. His response was, "We did not teach our daughter that."

One of the two statements is a lie, and a lie needs to be corrected. When he told me in my car that he and his wife never taught their daughter not to date Blacks, I said to him, "You said it publicly, and you have to go back and clean it up. If not, when am I supposed to believe you? How do I know when you are telling me the truth or telling me a lie?"

All we wanted him to do was for him to say publicly, in the same context as he had made the original statement, "You know what? I lied. I repent of it. I said that on the tape, but we really didn't train our daughter that way; we really didn't teach her that way."

When I wrote to his father, I explained:

> All we wanted [him] to say was I don't care if the races mix; it doesn't matter to God and it certainly doesn't matter to me.

I did not like the breach between our ministry and theirs; I wanted it healed with all my heart. But not getting a retraction from the son, how could I help but feel that he truly believed the races should not mix?

To me, the fact that he was dwelling on this at all appeared to be a sign of racism. In my experience, interracial couples marry because they have something in common, because they are compatible in their personalities and values. They may have met each other in school or at work or in a social situation, and however they met, they were not necessarily looking for a person of another color. There aren't many black people who wake up in the ghetto and say, "Oh, you know what? Today I'm going to Beverly Hills and find a white woman to marry." Regardless of where people live or work, most people are not on the hunt to find somebody of another ethnicity.

I don't care who my son marries. I would only counsel him this way: "You're saved, so she ought to be saved; you're filled with the Holy Spirit and speak with tongues, so she ought to be filled with the Holy Spirit and speak with tongues; you're a tither, she should be a tither, or you're going to have a spiritual conflict." I do not care if he marries a Black, White, Asian, Native American or any combination thereof. Whatever woman he chooses is up to him; I won't have to live with her, he will. Of course I will have to deal with the grandchildren, but I will love them whatever color they are and whatever color their mother is. I don't have a problem with mixing races, and I can say it publicly. I could not understand why the son of the head of the ministry could not also say it publicly, unless it was not in his heart to say it. His unwillingness to recant and repent continued the appearance that he was a racist.

In my letter to his father, I quoted the son's statement:

> I don't think that we oughta to mix any of the races. That's my opinion, okay?"

Then I explained to his father:

> ... If you listen to the tape, [he] makes these statements
>
> with apparent forethought and [deliberate] inflections in his voice. However, when he said he didn't mean them, then I was satisfied and simply requested that he retract and recant them....

The son and father apparently felt that Betty and I wanted the son to say that he was a racist. I did not want him to say that, unless that is who he is. I would hope that he is not, and that he would say that he is not. But again, it appeared that he was. The way to change that appearance was to do it within the same format as the original impression was created.

> We believed this to be very simple [I continued to his father], so you can imagine that when he declared to us with your concurrence that he would not do this, we were left with no other alternative than to believe that maybe he and perhaps you were racist, since he was unwilling to say, "I am not a racist, even if my words sounded like I was."
>
> At that point, we withdrew, as the Bible says to avoid the appearance of evil. We felt that to continue the fellowship with you, with no reconciliation of the statements, would be to send a very disturbing message to the Body of Christ, and especially to those of color who view me, as I said in an earlier letter, as someone they look up to, as a leader. If they saw me continue to associate with you, with no retraction of those statements by [him], then I believe my integrity as a man of God would have been compromised.

Before continuing with my letter to the head of the ministry, I would like to clarify some of the events that had transpired at my own ministry, Crenshaw Christian Center, concerning this issue. I had played the tape for the members of my executive board, because they, along with me, make decisions about how the church's money is to be spent. At that time, my ministry had committed to sowing into the other ministry one hundred thousand dollars a year to help support it. But as I saw it, if you have a problem with my son marrying your daughter, you have a problem with spending my money. How could someone be a person of integrity and take black people's money while viewing them as inferior? I could not have sat in that boardroom and sent our money to support a ministry that had that kind of attitude.

Up to that time, the ministry in question had had an annual convocation for twenty years. My wife and I had been to eighteen of them. Not only did we go, but I had been the only black speaker, with one exception (one year they had a special program, and they had two other black speakers, a husband and wife who were graduates of their school of ministry).

Since 1993, when we withdrew fellowship, they have had a black speaker every year except for the year we withdrew. I had been invited to be a speaker at that convocation, and I declined, saying that I could not speak until the issue was resolved, because my black brethren who view me as a leader would see it as if I were in agreement with those who had apparently taken a racist view. That year, they had three black speakers. I felt they were trying to camouflage the situation with window dressing, three token Blacks instead of one white minister recanting racist statements.

I called the three speakers on the phone and asked them if they knew about the tape. In essence, they told me, "Well, it really doesn't matter."

It matters to me. Their way of thinking keeps them under the thumb of the system, the old racist system that had been instituted in the days of slavery. It was still working: I had been the house nigger, and now the field niggers were running into the house to take my place. As much as I wanted to speak at that convocation, because it was a tremendous opportunity to be able to disseminate the Word to a great number of people from all over the world, I could not go there to speak.

I was not going to sell my people down the river. I am black and I am going to stay black and I am going to stand with black. I am not against anyone, but for once in our lifetimes Blacks must stand together instead of trying to please the white man. That is the game that has been played against us from the days of slavery. That is how we have been kept docile; that is how we have been kept in slavery—physical, economic and mental slavery—by dividing us and keeping us apart. Apparently, some of us are still so anxious to have the white man's approval that even now we will sell our own brothers and sisters down the river.

I had a meeting with members of my congregation who regularly attended the convocation. Many started going there because of Betty and me. I played the tape and told them that I couldn't go. "I have to take a stand," I told them, "and I am not telling you not to support that ministry. I am simply telling you why I can no longer do so, so that when the lies start circulating, you will have heard it firsthand from your pastor, not from some ninth-hand source." I did not tell anyone not to go; that was not my purpose. I made it clear they had to make their own decisions about attendance.

As a result of that meeting, some of our members called or wrote letters to the ministry and told them to take their names off their mailing list. They felt they could no longer support the ministry after hearing the tape. For these people, too, it was a matter of principle; that is why this issue must be dealt with out in the open, because the lie cannot continue.

Returning to the final letter I wrote to the father of the minister on the tape, in it I told him:

> Lastly, I have attached copies of letters [sent to] two of our members, wherein [your son] made statements that were disturbing to me. They are as follows:

> ... Both [my father] and I have talked to Brother Fred Price about this situation, but he has chosen not to accept my apologies.

I must comment on this before going any further. I, as a man of God, do not have any choice but to forgive someone or I hinder my own blessings. I cannot be the pastor of Crenshaw Christian Center and be such a fool as to hold something in my heart and not forgive.

It was never about apology. I forgave him the moment he said, "We're so sorry that we hurt you." I told him, "Apology accepted, but we have to deal with this situation. We have to fix it. There is no way in the world that I can hold anything against you, but what about the tape of your sermon? You've got to correct the statements you made."

It was astonishing to me that since I had never had a problem accepting his apology, he would write a letter on his ministry's letterhead telling members of my congregation that I would not accept it. That was another lie that needed to be corrected publicly because it was sent out publicly.

I concluded the letter to his father by saying:

> The Word admonishes us to lie not to one another, so this concerned me. I told [your son] that day in the car that I forgave him, when he asked me to, so this statement is not truthful. Furthermore, in the same conversation, I told [him] that this was not an issue of forgiveness for me anyway, as he had not done anything to me, personally. He told me that he viewed me differently. Our relationship was not at stake or in jeopardy.
>
> I will be honest with you. I would love to get this situation righted, because Betty and I do very much miss the fellowship we once shared with you. It is my earnest desire to resolve this matter, but there are principles involved here that I stand for, and that I believe the Bible also

supports. So my prayer is that illumination will come after you have read this letter. I anxiously and prayerfully await your response. Love in Christ, Fred.

The father—the head of the ministry that had distributed his son's tape all over the world—never responded to this letter. After a while, I called him, and, once again, received no satisfactory response. A white minister from another church wrote to the son on his own in support of my position, but his heartfelt words also produced no communication.[1] As a result, the breach continues to this day. Betty and I miss the fellowship of that ministry, but the leader's son has still never repented for or recanted the statements he made that:

1. he taught his daughter not to date Blacks;
2. he believes that the different races should not marry;
3. Brother Price has never accepted his apology.

I am standing for a principle, and I am sorry to see that many of my black brethren have flocked from the field to the house, letting Massa know that everything Massa does is all right. "Just keep doing what you're doing, it's okay with us"—that's the message they are sending. And of course if you get enough people to accept that, the question then becomes, "Who is Fred Price? Forget him, we can just keep on doing business as usual because we have all these other people supporting us, and it doesn't seem to bother them."

I am not going to be pushed down and walked on. People have walked on us for 380 years, and that is 380 years too long.

---

[1] This minister's letter to me and his letter to the minister who delivered the message against interracial marriage are in Appendix A.

8

People's Concerns

I believe that the Lord has raised me up for a time like this: to be, as it were, a catalyst to find the solution to what I consider to be America's biggest challenge—and the Church's biggest challenge—the issue of race. I believe that the Lord has called me to be a watchman on the wall. Ezekiel 3:17 says:

> **"Son of man, I have made you a watchman for the house of Israel; therefore hear a word from My mouth, and give them warning from Me."**

And Jeremiah 1:10 states:

> **"See, I have this day set you over the nations and over the kingdoms, to root out and to pull down, to destroy and to throw down, to build and to plant."**

I believe that is my assignment.

I want to share a letter that I received after I began to teach about racism and talk publicly about the incident that had happened to me with the minister and his father. It is a positive letter, and I appreciate the people who wrote it. I feel the love that exudes from it. I'd like you to read it and take note of the questions it asks:

Greetings in the name of our Lord Jesus Christ.

My husband and I have been ardent listeners to your TV program since 1985 and we have been tremendously blessed due to your preaching and teaching of faith through the Word. We would like to commend you for your sincerity and uprightness and for your courage to continue despite all the odds. We know that God will continue to bless you and your family as you so richly deserve. However, Pastor Price, as much as we share with you that deep passion to bring the sordid practice of "racism in the church" as a series on the air, we are very deeply concerned as to the repercussions this may have on you, your family, church members and other devoted TV members, who have been supporting you without ever doubting your trustworthiness and loyalty to God and men. Pastor Price, please read and view this letter as one of the most sincere expressions of love and admiration and concern for you and caring from the bottom of our hearts. We have prayed about the "racism" which you are about to address and we would like to know that you are approaching this dilemma with all the conviction that you are doing this at the right time: So we would like you to answer these very important questions, which we hope would dispel any doubts or uncertainties by you and us, before the commencement of the series. We strongly support you, but we feel compelled to know that you are very ready to lay "the assault!"

Questions are, 1: Are you doing this for personal conviction or as a vendetta against persons who betrayed your trust in them? 2: Are you sure beyond doubt that you are ready for this tremendous task? 3: Are you aware of and prepared for the negative effects, possible tragic consequences, this may have on you and your family and the church? 4: Do you have the wholehearted support in this of your wife, children, in-laws, close and trusted members and supporters of your ministry? Brother Price,

> we know that our faith is not as strong as yours in all matters, but if you can from the bottom of your heart with all of your being answer these questions truthfully and positively, we will be satisfied that you are ready. If you have any doubts, please let us all call upon the Lord together so that He will further strengthen you and all of us your beloved supporters in Christ, that salvation shall bring us that victory we have so long sought. Dr. Price, we admire and respect you and your family very much and we only wish for God to continue to guide you and bless you in all matters. God's blessings to you and your entire family. We hope you would share this letter with them. May your faith be so strong that through your teaching of the Word, we would one day trust the Lord without reservations.
>
> In the service of the King,
> [Name withheld]

I am grateful for this letter and understand the concern from which it came, and I would like to answer the questions, starting with the first:

> Are you doing this for personal conviction or as a vendetta against persons who betrayed your trust in them?

If I were a person who allowed himself to be hurt, I would be deeply hurt by this question. It is sad to me that any person would think that I was taking on this task for revenge against anybody; for me, it has always been about principle. I am doing it because I have been commissioned by Jesus to do it.

Question number two asks:

> Are you sure beyond doubt that you are ready for this tremendous task?

I would never have started it if I were not ready.

Question number three asks:

Are you aware of and prepared for the negative effects, possible tragic consequences, this may have on you and your family and the church?

I think that there will be a great sigh of relief from many people that they did not have to get the assignment but that someone else is dealing with it. I am not concerned about any tragic consequences.

Question number four asks:

Do you have the wholehearted support in this of your wife, children, in-laws, close and trusted members and supporters of your ministry?

I don't need it. I am not doing this because I have my wife's support. If my wife told me not to do this, I would tell her what Job told his wife in Job 2:10:

But he said to her, "You speak as one of the foolish women speaks…."

God put this in my heart to do. He would not give me a message without having people to hear it. I know my ministry is with me and I know my family is with me, but I am not doing it because they are. I am doing it because I have an assignment and because it is the right thing to do.

I sincerely appreciate the letter-writers' love for me, and perhaps others have had the same concerns, but I would say to everyone who has these concerns, **… He who is in you is greater than he who is in the world** (1 John 4:4). With God on my side, I have nothing to fear.

Paul tells us in Ephesians 5:11:

And have no fellowship with the unfruitful works of darkness, but rather expose them.

That is actually every Christian's call. Works of darkness should be exposed, and racism is darkness developed out of the very pit of hell. It needs to be exposed.

Paul asks a very pointed question in Galatians 4:16:

Have I therefore become your enemy because I tell you the truth?

People do not want to deal with the issue underlying racism, the fact that prejudice against black people is based on our supposed inferiority. By telling the truth about this, why should I become anyone's enemy?

The following is a letter from a black person.

Dear Pastor Price,

... Another thing, why is it that you have this desire to have your son marry a white woman? I have never heard any white pastor get up on worldwide TV and promote the idea that it is okay to marry anyone black. Why do you have to be so "liberal" and out of touch?! Whenever you talk this way I can't help but feel you wished you had the opportunity to marry a white woman. I believe you would if this was 20 years hence, or if you had a chance now you would. This is not disrespectful to your wife, Betty, because you could never find a white woman like her.

I love the biblical messages you teach, but please take note of what you say when it comes to your son marrying white women or African-Americans marrying out of their race. If anything you should be teaching Blacks to love one another more. Subliminal messages are what you are giving your son and others who are not aware of the subtle brainwashing you're doing. I'm not sure if even you are aware of this. Please stop it! Another thing, you were going to teach on race and why one race (white) thinks they are so much better than anyone else. This I agree with you on. Everyone knows they feel this way.

Truly yours,
A faithful viewer

I want to address the question, "Can my son marry your white daughter?" Have you ever heard the term *acid test*? It is a test that jewelers use to find out whether something is gold and, if so, what degree of gold it is. Each degree has a slightly different color. Twenty-four-karat gold is pure gold, and it has a certain color. Eighteen-karat gold is not as pure; it is mixed with an alloy, and it has another color. Fourteen-karat gold is even less pure. As a test, jewelers apply nitric acid to the gold. If it is real gold, it will show its color; if it is not, it bubbles up and turns green.

When I ask a white person, "Can my son marry your daughter?" that is *my acid test* to see if he or she is a racist. If people are not racists, they will say, "Fine! As long as the kids love each other and all things are equal, I don't care."

As I've said, I am not advocating that my son marry anyone of any particular color, but the question is my acid test. It is the only question I have been able to come up with to ask white people—because white people are the ones who have the problem with race. Of course not all white people have this problem, but if they do, the problem is with intermarrying.

If I ask someone, "Can my son marry your daughter?" and that person hesitates, then he or she has a problem. If you ask me, "Can your daughter marry my son?" my answer would be, without hesitation, "Yes, if they love each other, and all other things are equal, I don't have a problem with it."

Some people may have a problem and not even realize it until they are asked this question or until they ask it of themselves.

Please don't misunderstand me; people have a right to their preferences. But when you have a problem in your heart with intermarriage, so much so that it scares you, then you have a real problem. That is why the white churches moved out of the inner cities and into the suburbs. It is why they raised millions of dollars to send white missionaries all the way across the world to the darkest, blackest Africa to win those heathens to Christ but they neglected the heathens in the inner city.

The remarks that the black woman made in her letter—that I want to marry a white woman—are ignorant. I am already married to the best woman on the planet; I have been married for more than forty-six years, and if the letter-writer thinks I am going to trade in my wife for any woman of any color, she does not know who my wife is or who I am.

9

The Bible's Acid Test

White prejudice against Blacks has been part of this nation's cultural fabric from the beginning. It can be overt, and it can be subtle. You do not have to want to marry a person of color in order to not be a racist. But if you are a white person, I would like you to look within yourself to see if you have a way of viewing different races in a negative way that you may not have been aware of—a way that has been passed down to you, perhaps indirectly, by your parents, by their parents and by their parents.

Racial prejudice, as I've pointed out, is not genetically transmitted, it is socially transmitted by word of mouth. It cannot possibly come from the Spirit of God. It has to come from the spirit of Satan, because the Scripture tells us that God has made out of one blood everyone to dwell on the face of the earth. That is why, as I said earlier, it is a scientific and medical fact that, all things being equal regarding blood type, all blood is interchangeable.

Here is the Bible's acid test. Second Corinthians 6:14-16 contains the only Scripture in the New Testament about who we are and who we should be joined with:

> **Do not be unequally yoked together with unbelievers. For what fellowship has righteousness with lawlessness? And what communion has light with darkness?**

> **And what accord has Christ with Belial? Or what part has a believer with an unbeliever?**
>
> **And what agreement has the temple of God with idols? For you are the temple of the living God. As God has said: "I will dwell in them and walk among them. I will be their God, and they shall be My people."**

Notice that it says, **And what agreement has the temple of God with idols? For you are the temple of the living God.** I have a question: When the Lord says, "You are the temple of the living God," is He talking only to the white part of the Body of Christ? Or is He talking to the black, red, yellow and brown parts as well?

There is a passage of Scripture that I first heard many years ago. It is found in John 3:16. It says:

> **"For God so loved the world...."**

How would you define "the world"? White? Black? Red? Yellow? Brown?

> **"For God so loved the world that He gave His only begotten Son, that whoever believes...."**

I am a "whoever." I just happen to be black. Another whoever just happens to be white. But God said *whoever,* so whoever has to include black, white, red, yellow or brown. If I am the temple of God, and you are the temple of God, then why can't we marry, even though our exteriors may be different shades?

I've said it before: If black people are inferior, then God is inferior, because God made black people. There is not one black person on this planet who made himself or herself black. Nor is there one white person on this planet who made himself or herself white; nor one red, yellow or brown person who made himself or herself red, yellow or brown. Since God created all of us, God must have made us the color we are. And if it is all right with God to have human beings of different colors, it should be all right with everyone else.

The Scripture tells us:

Do not be unequally yoked together with unbelievers....

That is the only restriction for Believers. It has nothing to do with color; it is about Believers being connected with unbelievers. If a white unbeliever marries a white Believer, they are unequally yoked; if a red, black, yellow or brown Believer marries a correspondingly colored unbeliever, they are unequally yoked. So if I am to be equally yoked, I may marry any Believer of any color.

It is about Believers and unbelievers, righteousness and lawlessness. We, as Believers, are the righteousness of God; unbelievers—non-Christians—are considered by God as non-righteous or unrighteous. As the traditional *King James* Bible asks in 2 Corinthians 6:14:

... And what communion hath light with darkness?

This is not talking about black and white as colors: It is talking about knowledge and lack of knowledge.

Verse 15 says:

And what concord hath Christ with Belial?...

Belial represents Satan—and Christ, of course, represents the Son of God. In this context, Christ also represents us—or we represent Him. If I am a member in the Body of Christ, then I am Christ; I am not Christ by myself, the Son of God, but I am a part of Christ, so in that sense I am Christ. My right hand is as much Fred Price as my left hand is. Why? Because it is attached to the same body. Because we are in Christ, we are Christ. That is how the Father God sees us: If I am the Body of Christ, then I am a cell, if you would, in the Body of Christ.

Joining with another in marriage has nothing whatsoever to do with race; the only restriction is against joining Believers with unbelievers. If we adopt any other restriction than this, we are wrong; if we use any justification other than this for why two people cannot come together, then we are missing God.

10

Addressing the Natural to Get to the Spiritual

I received a letter dated August 10, 1997, in which the writer made an interesting observation. I want to share it because I have a feeling there may be others who have had the same thoughts as the writer of the letter.

> I watched your program on Channel 9, the UPN station, this morning. You hit a responsive chord in me today when mentioning the need for a "Black minister" such as yourself to speak to the issue of Black folk despite the criticism of the Church at large. At one time, I did not think you were aware or cared about addressing such a need. I am glad to see it was a mistaken conclusion.

When I became a Christian, I found I was still faced with the problem of racism. As I mentioned, the night I got saved, the white minister who counseled me—and he was not just a minister, but a teacher in a Bible institute with his own radio program—told me that according to the Bible, the races should be segregated. And that was on the night I got saved! By saved, I mean that I accepted Jesus Christ as my personal Savior and Lord.

When I came into a knowledge of the Word many years later, I found out that in John 8:36, Jesus tells us:

"Therefore if the Son makes you free, you shall be free indeed."

Then I found this Scripture in John 8:31-32:

Then Jesus said to those Jews who believed Him, "If you abide in My word, you are My disciples indeed.

"And you shall know the truth, and the truth shall make you free."

Free of what? Free of anything that would hold us in bondage—physical bondage like sickness or disease, financial bondage like lack of money and other necessities, racial bondage, which includes all the effects of color and ethnic prejudice.

I got ahold of the Word and began to see how to walk (or live) by faith (what God's Word says). Instantly, I began to apply the principles that I had been exposed to. Everything was not fully developed instantly, but I could see change begin right away.

I continued to pursue the Word, and it changed my whole life. It brought me out of all kinds of phobias and fears—like fear of water and fear of flying. It set me free. The biggest freedom was freedom from financial problems. God, through His Word, began to work on my finances. It was not that He was not working on them before; it was that He could not work before, because I was not cooperating with Him.

I began to apply those principles in the church, to the FaithDome, and to the thousands who attend weekly; to the radio ministry and TV ministry, which have been airing consistently for more than twenty years. These are just some of the results of my getting ahold of the Word and walking by faith (living by God's Word) for more than thirty years.

My wife and I applied that Word to our family. At the time, our children were teenagers. They did not have the benefit of going to private school. They had to go to the same public schools as everyone else's kids. They were faced with drugs, illicit sex, smoking, drinking, partying, carousing, everything that other kids are faced with in public junior high and high schools. But we put the Word and the fear of God in them, and the Word worked like a charm. We never had one moment's trouble from our kids; I have never had to go to the police station or to the principal's office to pick up my child.

Having had this powerful experience of faith myself, I thought, "I don't need to deal with being black; I don't need to deal with racism; I don't need to deal with any of the issues associated with it. All I have to do is get the Word into people, and if they get this Word, they can rise above the circumstances of life. We did it. We did it, and it worked for us."

Then I was rudely awakened by the incident I've discussed regarding the ministers with whom I broke fellowship. That was when I found out that some people, regardless of how high they go spiritually, do not let God's Word interfere with their personal prejudices. That was when I realized, "I'll have to go back down and bring my brothers and sisters up. I have to reach people where they are, and show them how to come up."

Black, white, red, yellow or brown—whoever you are—you will still have to learn how to walk by faith, because you have an adversary called the devil. Regardless of your color, you will have to come to the place of learning to walk by faith if you are going to please God, because Hebrews 11:6 tells us:

...without faith it is impossible to please Him [God]**....**

The Bible does not say without white skin, or black skin, or brown, red or yellow skin; it says, **"...without faith it is impossible to please Him...."** So Christians will have to know how to walk by faith.

God knows exactly how to position the pawns on the chessboard, and He has positioned me perfectly, because I am in a place where no one can deny the success of the Word in my life or ministry. God has given me credibility. People may not like me and may stop listening to me and sending TV support, but they cannot deny that God is at work in this ministry. So I have gone the way God has led me.

Think about it: My ministry is located in what is called the ghetto—not in the suburbs, not in Beverly Hills, not in Century City. We are in the heart of Los Angeles; we are in the "hood." But look at what God has done with black skin in the ghetto! The FaithDome is the biggest church in Los Angeles, the biggest sanctuary in America—white, black, red, yellow or brown.

Not one single chicken sacrificed its life as a fund-raising meal to build the FaithDome and purchase the grounds—a $26 million project. We did it by faith! No gimmicks. No tricks. Just by teaching people to walk (live) by the Word.

So I have a platform from which to speak to the Body of Christ. We are right where some people said it could not be done. They said, "God has fled to the suburbs," because all the white people had left the inner city. But God is still here. And God has created a channel through which He can speak. I don't have any agenda but God's agenda. I want to please God more than anything else.

That is why I have walked the path I have walked. It is not that I have only now become interested in Blacks. That isn't the issue at all; it is the fact that many black people are so hung up because of the past and because of what has happened to them, that they cannot hear God when He tells them to walk by faith. They say, "Faith, yes, that sounds fine, but what about a job? What about this messed-up neighborhood I have to live in?"

First Corinthians 2:14 says:

> **But the natural man does not receive the things of the Spirit of God, for they are foolishness to him; nor can he know them, because they are spiritually discerned.**

Many black people cannot get up to the spiritual because they are so concerned with the natural—food, clothing, housing, jobs—that they have never realized that the spiritual can change the natural. Now I am going where they are so that they can understand where I am.

Let's look at 1 Corinthians 9:19-23.

> **For though I am free from all men, I have made myself a servant to all, that I might win the more;**
>
> **and to the Jews I became as a Jew, that I might win Jews; to those who are under the law, as under the law, that I might win those who are under the law;**
>
> **to those who are without law, as without law (not being without law toward God, but under law toward Christ), that I might win those who are without law;**
>
> **to the weak I became as weak, that I might win the weak. I have become all things to all men, that I might by all means save some.**
>
> **Now this I do for the gospel's sake, that I may be partaker of it with you.**

I have become very black so that I can win Blacks. Please understand that I have not become black to neglect anyone else, but in an attempt to bring black people to a place where they can understand that God truly loves them, and that God is no respecter of persons. It may look as if all of a sudden I have become interested in racism and its cruel effects on my own people, but I have always been interested; it's just that many people did not understand my interest, because they were looking for something else.

If you run into a man who is not a Christian but is starving to death, that is not the time to preach Jesus to him. Give the man something to eat, get his stomach full so his mind is not on his stomach, then he will be in a position to listen to what you have to say. When a man is dying of thirst, that is not the time to talk to him about being filled with the Holy Spirit. Get the man some water, get his thirst quenched, then he will be in a position to hear. I am talking about racism because I want our country to end racism once and for all, and because I want to reach people who have been starving and thirsty because of it.

Many Blacks have turned away from the Church because of the shameful actions and attitudes they have witnessed through the years. They have forgotten that it was because of Jesus and because of the Church—the true Church—that their forebears were able to make it through slavery. That was the only thing that kept them. It was not Muhammad who brought those slaves through; it was Jesus, their faith and trust in Christ.[1]

Many young people have left the Church because they thought that the Church was white and that it did not like Blacks. That image is in the process of being altered, and this book is one step toward altering it. Many black people have flooded into all kinds of "isms" that are going to consume them, and they will find themselves in hell. Someone has to reach those people, and that is part of my assignment.

In Luke 19:1-10, we find another illustration of what I'm saying:

> **Then Jesus entered and passed through Jericho.**
>
> **Now behold, there was a man named Zacchaeus who was a chief tax collector, and he was rich.**

---

[1] See Roy E. Finkenbine, "Culture and Religion in the Quarters," *Sources of the African-American Past: Primary Sources in American History* (New York: Longman Publishers, Inc., 1997), 47-53. Randolph states, "Whites used Christianity to socialize slaves to work hard, be honest and obedient, and accept their situation. But slaves forged a faith more suited for their needs. Meeting secretly in swamps, woods, brush arbors, and slave cabins of southern farms and plantations, they created a variation of the Christianity they had received—one that helped them endure slavery and often preached the values of freedom and virtues of resistance."

And he sought to see who Jesus was, but could not because of the crowd, for he was of short stature.

So he ran ahead and climbed up into a sycamore tree to see Him, for He was going to pass that way.

And when Jesus came to the place, He looked up and saw him, and said to him, "Zacchaeus, make haste and come down, for today I must stay at your house."

So he made haste and came down, and received Him joyfully.

But when they saw it, they all complained, saying, "He has gone to be a guest with a man who is a sinner."

Then Zacchaeus stood and said to the Lord, "Look, Lord, I give half of my goods to the poor; and if I have taken anything from anyone by false accusation, I restore fourfold."

And Jesus said to him, "Today salvation has come to this house, because he also is a son of Abraham;

"for the Son of Man has come to seek and to save that which was lost."

Many black people in America have lost their way, and it is time for them to find it. They have lost their way because of the dust clouds of racism and slavery, and a lack of knowledge about themselves. They are in a fog, not sure where they are, and it has shown in their actions. They are misbehaving because they do not really know who they are. In order to find out who they are, we have to go back into our history.

People have said to me, "That's unpleasant. Let's forget about the past." We cannot forget about what we have never known, and, as I've pointed out, most of us black people do not know our past; in essence, we do not really have a past. And that is part of our problem.

Some people will reject this message because they will say that I am not coming across in love. They think I should speak out with less passion. I am not going to do that, because I am angry—angry about the fact that racism could not have existed without the consent of the Church, and angry that the Church as a whole has done nothing to stop it. I do not do anything unless I can substantiate it by the Bible, and my anger is Bible-based. Earlier, I mentioned the story of Jesus and the man with the withered hand. Mark 3:1-5 tells us:

> **And He entered the synagogue again, and a man was there who had a withered hand.**
>
> **So they watched Him closely, whether He would heal him on the Sabbath, so that they might accuse Him.**
>
> **And He said to the man who had the withered hand, "Step forward."**
>
> **Then He said to them, "Is it lawful on the Sabbath to do good or to do evil, to save life or to kill?" But they kept silent.**
>
> **And when He had looked around at them with anger, being grieved by the hardness of their hearts, He said to the man, "Stretch out your hand." And he stretched it out, and his hand was restored as whole as the other.**

Jesus was angry because the Pharisees in the temple were so concerned about maintaining the status quo that they did not care about the man with the withered hand. All they wanted was to maintain the tradition of Sabbath, not to see the man healed. This grieved Jesus, and He was righteously indignant.

That is the kind of anger that I have. I am grieved that the Church—the Church of the Lord Jesus Christ (or the so-called Church of the Lord Jesus Christ)—has let the problem of racism fester and boil all these years, and has never really addressed it; that the Church, in fact, has perpetuated it by not speaking out. If the whole church world—and most of the church world is white—had spoken out against racism and racial, ethnic and color prejudice, what a difference it could have made!

But the Church as a whole does not care about black people. They want Blacks to get saved, of course, but for what purpose I don't really know. Maybe they believe that there is going to be a segregated heaven, perhaps a ghetto and a suburb section. I don't think so, because if there is, I am not going; I have had enough of racism while I have been here. I don't want to spend eternity in the same kind of environment.

Again, I am not saying that every white Christian has this attitude, but too many do. If Whites really cared about Blacks, they would not have fled the inner cities, nor would they have made us pay a fortune for the grossly overpriced property they left behind.

When my wife and I first got married more than forty-six years ago, we as black people could not rent an apartment in the area where our church is situated. From downtown Los Angeles to 103rd Street in Watts, black people simply could not rent. Forty years ago, I tried again and again. Then, when Whites finally decided that too many Blacks were applying to get in, they left, and they left the whole neighborhood, including the property where the church is located, like a dump. Normally, people fix up property and sell it, but the white people who owned these properties allowed them to deteriorate, and sold them in terrible condition.

When we built the FaithDome, we had to hook up with the Los Angeles sewer system, and we discovered that to do it, it would cost a great deal of money. The reason for this was that the previous owners had violations that the city did not charge them for. From my understanding, some time before we bought the property along the Vermont Corridor where our church is located, each property owner was supposed to have paid a certain amount for improvements in the sewer system. Apparently, the previous owners of the grounds had not paid for these improvements, and had gotten away scot-free.

When we bought the property and decided to build the Faith-Dome, we had to get city approval to use the sewer system. The city charged us a $200,000 penalty fee, which should have been paid by the previous owners, and which the previous owners knew should have been paid before we bought the property.

That is cold-blooded. The previous owners knew that no white people were going to buy the property, that it would be bought either by Hispanics or Blacks, and their attitude was, "Let them pay through the nose!" Two hundred thousand dollars just to hook up to the sewer system—all of which should have been paid by the people who occupied the property when the improvements along the Vermont Corridor were originally made. But the government is like God. They let you go on your merry way because Judgment Day is coming. The city said to us, "You want to hook up? Fine! No problem! But you're going to have to hook us up first—with $200,000. Then we'll hook you up."

In a way, the government did the same thing when it gave Blacks emancipation.

First, the government permitted black people to be taken from their native land, made into slaves and stripped of their heritage and family ties, so that they could not find agreement and strength with each other. The government made it perfectly legal for black fathers to be sold off in one direction, their wives sold off in another and their children sold off in another, breaking all family bonds and breaking generations and generations of black hearts.

So-called Christians did this—but they could not have been Christians: They could not have known God and done any of these things. They kept Blacks in bondage from 1619 until 1865 and worked them until they dropped dead, because there were plenty more in Africa; they did not even keep them healthy, they just let them die and bought some more.

Then, after all of this, in 1865, the government gave Blacks emancipation. Think about it: From 1619 until 1865, black people were taken from Africa, made into slaves and taught absolutely nothing. The majority of them could not read, could not write, barely could speak the language. Then the government opened the gate and set them free, and acted amazed because they did not compete with Whites. They could not read—because for all those years it was against the law to teach a Black to read![2] The wonderful, good, precious, honest white Christians who did teach their slaves to read did it at the risk of their own lives. How could Blacks act civilized when they had been treated like animals for more than two centuries and then suddenly turned loose?

Much of what is going on today stems directly from that past. Many Blacks act the way they do because they do not know any

---

[2] For information about the code prohibiting Whites from teaching slaves to read, see Carter A. Wilson, *Racism: From Slavery to Advanced Capitalism* (Thousand Oaks, California: Sage Publications, 1996), 67. Also see Byron Farwell, *Stonewall: A Biography of General Thomas J. Jackson* (New York: W.W. Norton & Co., Inc., 1992), 125-126,196. Farwell points out that, besides not being allowed to be taught, in the aftermath of Nat Turner's slave rebellion in Virginia in 1831, black people were not even allowed by law to assemble or be assembled as a body. Jackson, who as a deacon of a Presbyterian church in Lexington, Virginia, taught a Sunday school for Blacks before the Civil War, fell afoul of this rule. Colonel Samuel McDowell Reid and two lawyers, William McLaughlin and J.D. Davidson, confronted him in front of the city courthouse about the school being an "unlawful assembly." When told by Davidson that the grand jury would probably test the viability of the school in the light of the statute, Jackson angrily replied, "Sir, if you were, as you should be, a Christian man, you would not think or say so." When Davidson protested, Jackson turned and left. The two men apologized to each other shortly afterwards and the school evidently stayed open, since Jackson continued to send monetary donations for it during the war.

better; they do not know their history. They do not know that their heritage has been purposely stripped away from them, and they act out of keeping with their true heritage.[3]

If relations between the races remain as they are now, white people will merely continue running out to the suburbs—and if too many Blacks move to the suburbs, Whites will move again and create new suburbs. And every time they do that, they are telling us, "We do not want you to be with us."

Again, I am not talking about everyone; I am talking about general patterns. You know if your heart is right and if you don't hate black people. My daddy had an old saying: "If you throw an old shoe into a pack of dogs, the only dog that hollers and screams is the one that got hit." So if you are the dog that got hit, you should holler, but if you are not the dog that got hit, don't worry about it.

I am grieved just as Jesus was grieved, grieved because all of this could have been averted.

Let's look at Mark 11:15-17:

> **So they came to Jerusalem. Then Jesus went into the temple and began to drive out those who bought and sold in the temple, and overturned the tables of the money changers and the seats of those who sold doves.**
>
> **And He would not allow anyone to carry wares through the temple.**
>
> **Then He taught, saying to them, "Is it not written, 'My house shall be called a house of prayer for all nations'? But you have made it a 'den of thieves.' "**

---

[3] Black people have a wonderful heritage that is thousands of years old, and in Part Two of this book, I will look at the stripping away of black culture during slavery and at the black heritage that most of us, Black and White, are not aware of.

This is Jesus. He is talking to the people of His day, in the place where God was supposed to be reverenced and honored—the temple. And they had turned it into a den of thieves. Jesus became righteously indignant. I believe He is righteously indignant today. But He is not here in person, so His righteous indignation has to be manifested through the vessels that He chooses to represent Him. I am one of them.

If you have thought I am not acting in love, I hope you will understand now that if I did not love everyone, then I would not do what I am doing.

I love God, I love the Church I am part of, I love people of all nations, and I have seen what the sin of racism has been doing to the Church and to our country. Everyone suffers as a result of it. I love my people, and I attempted for years to give them the Word. Many of them got it, and it has changed their lives. This is not the white man's religion; that is the lie that has been disseminated through the centuries. This is God's Word for everyone who is willing to receive it.

In Ephesians 4:26, it says:

"Be angry, and do not sin": do not let the sun go down on your wrath.

The word *angry* means righteous indignation. It means that when things are not right, we ought to be angry about it; we ought to be angry about that which is unrighteous.

How could a preacher, a supposed minister of the Gospel, stand by and watch a family offered up for sale on the auction block like cows, sheep or goats? How could the Church stand by silently while a black father was auctioned to the highest bidder, while his wife, with their little children clinging to her torn clothes, watched him being taken away in chains, knowing that none of them would ever have the possibility of seeing him again? How could a preacher, a man who claimed to know God, stand by and watch such horror?

How could a preacher, a minister of the Gospel, of the Church, let a man come to church and sit there and take communion—when the man has just taken a black slave who spoke up for his rights and beaten him with a whip until he died.[4] If a white man had done that to another white man, he would have been hanged. But a black man was an animal, so killing him was as acceptable as shooting a dog. You sell him, you buy him, you rip up his family and rape his woman, sell his kids, use them for slaves, use up their lives. You don't give them medication or take care of them, because it doesn't matter—you just go down to the auction block after church and buy another slave.

This is history! Many white people don't know this, but it was their ancestors who did that.

---

[4] See John W. Blassingame, ed., *Slave Testimony: Two Centuries of Letters, Speeches, Interviews, and Autobiographies* (Baton Rouge: Louisiana State University Press, 1977), 126. Several slaves' narratives in this book allude to the fact that Christian slave owners openly dehumanized and mistreated their slaves. One ex-slave states: "I have seen a Christian professor, after the communion, have four slaves tied together, and whipped raw, and then washed with beef brine." Also see Frederick Douglass, *Narrative of the Life of Frederick Douglass* (New York: Dover Publications, Inc., 1995), 46. Douglass, a former slave who became a leader of the abolitionist movement, and later fought to include Blacks as field soldiers in the Union Army during the Civil War, states: "I assert most unhesitatingly, that religion of the South is a mere covering for the most horrid crimes–a justifier of the most appalling brutality–a sanctifier of the most hateful frauds–and a dark shelter under which the darkest and foulest, grossest, and most infernal deeds of slave holders find the strongest protection. Were I to begin again reduced to the chains of slavery, next to that enslavement, I should regard being a slave of a religious master the greatest calamity that could befall me. For with all slave holders with whom I have met, religious slave holders are the worst. I have ever found them the meanest and the basest, the most cruel and cowardly, of all others."

I am not mad at the people who did this. They were ignorant people who apparently did not know any better. They certainly did not know God or they could not have treated humans like that. But the Church was *supposed* to know God. Church people *should* have known better. And they just sat silently by and said, "Praise the Lord, hallelujah." Slavery never could have existed without the Church. We ought to get angry, righteously indignant about it.

I am righteously indignant about the Church disgracing the Lord Jesus like that.

The Bible says, **"For God so loved the world...."** It does not say He loved the white man or the red man or the black man or the yellow man or the brown man. He loved the world. Everyone is precious in His sight. He created us all. How do you think He feels? Whites sat there in their lily-white superiority and let a man beat another man to death, for no other reason than that he talked back to the boss—and the Church let this go on for two-and-a-half centuries. And even today the Church is basically still racist.

Churches still go out to the suburbs and build beautiful cathedrals and collect millions of dollars to send missionaries halfway around the world to minister to black Africans, and here in our own country, we have people dying every day in the ghetto without Christ!

Why don't they send a missionary to the ghetto if they care so much for black people?

Part Two

1

Man's Origin: A Scientific View

There are two primary views of where people come from, the scientific and the biblical. First, let's look at the scientific viewpoint. The *Encyclopedia Americana* tells us:

> The theory of biological, or Darwinian, evolution, first announced in 1859, has been abundantly confirmed by an avalanche of data. Charles Darwin and Alfred Wallace postulated that all life on earth descended from a primordial cell and that life changed and proliferated due to chance mutations.[1]

The basis of the scientific view, then, is that life began as one cell and evolved into the different forms we know today through chance mutations.

The *Encyclopedia Americana* also explains:

> Another striking characteristic of life, also observable to human eyes that are in front of a thoughtful human brain, is the extraordinary degree of complexity and of organization in living creatures. A close examination of

---

[1] "Evolution of Life" *Encyclopedia Americana, International Edition*, v. 17 (Danbury, Connecticut: Grolier Limited, 1979), 424.

> flowers, insects, or mammals shows an almost incredibly precise arrangement of parts.[2]

This sounds remarkably like Psalm 139:14, which says we are **"fearfully and wonderfully made...."**

The scientific view goes on to say:

> This arrangement appears unchanged in countless individuals of a given species. It relates structure to function—that is, the right parts almost invariably appear in the right places. The leaves of the tree are not found below ground nor its roots up in its branches. This necessary-for-life organization is of a complexity simply not found in nonliving systems.[3]

Scientists recognize the complexity and precision of nature, yet they say it is all derived from chance—and that all life started with one cell, by chance. This is what makes it very different from the biblical view.

---

[2] "Complexity and Organization," *Encyclopedia Americana, International Edition*, v. 17, 418.

[3] "Complexity and Organization," 418.

2

Man's Origin: A Biblical View

The terms *complexity* and *organization* mentioned in the scientific viewpoint seem to indicate that there is an intelligent mind at work. Scientists themselves tell us that everything seems to be in the right place. Given this, I don't understand how science can say that all of this—all of life—in its complexity and organization got here through chance mutations.

Where did you come from? How did you get here? I believe the Bible is the only source that confirms that there was, and is, an intelligent mind behind all of this.

Genesis 1:1 says:

In the beginning God created the heavens and the earth.

That is an awesome statement. But it is easier for me to believe that God created heaven and earth than to believe that my ability to see in color and in three dimensions has evolved through chance mutations. It is easier for me to believe because that would indicate to me that an intelligent mind has put all of this together.

Genesis 1:11-12 tells us:

Then God said, "Let the earth bring forth grass, the herb that yields seed, and the fruit tree that yields

fruit according to its kind, whose seed is in itself, on the earth"; and it was so.

And the earth brought forth grass, the herb that yields seed according to its kind, and the tree that yields fruit, whose seed is in itself according to its kind. And God saw that it was good.

The scientific view says that everything came from one primordial cell; the biblical perspective diverges from this.

Let's look again at Genesis 1:1:

In the beginning God created the heavens and the earth.

Now let's review Verse 11:

Then God said, "Let the earth bring forth grass, the herb that yields seed, and the fruit tree that yields fruit according to its kind....

Its *kind*—that is the key concept; the Bible is saying that one cell cannot produce a man and a dog and a fish and a bird because a man and a dog and a fish and a bird are not of the same *kind.*

Verse 21 says:

So God created great sea creatures and every living thing that moves, with which the waters abounded, according to their kind, and every winged bird according to its kind. And God saw that it was good.

Verse 24 goes on to say:

Then God said, "Let the earth bring forth the living creature according to its kind: cattle and creeping thing and beast of the earth, each according to its kind"; and it was so.

The Bible tells us that God created everything that moves, and that He said that everything produces after its kind. It is absolutely scientifically validated by the facts that everything does produce according to its kind. I don't care what type of apple you cross with another type of apple, it will still produce an apple. It may be a redder apple, a yellower apple, a sweeter apple, a bigger apple, a seedless apple, an apple full of seeds, but it will still be an apple.

You can crossbreed dogs, and come out with a short dog, a long dog, a dog with long ears, a dog with short ears, a pointed-snout dog, a stubby-nosed dog, a long-legged dog, a short-legged dog, a spotted dog, a white dog, a black dog, a brown dog—but all are still dogs. You can do the same with horses. And guess what? You can crossbreed all humans, black ones with white ones, red ones with yellow ones, yellow ones with brown ones, and you will still get another human.

Everything produces after its kind. You don't get animals from humans and you don't get humans from animals. You don't get birds from fish, and you don't get fish from birds. Scientists want us to believe that this is all by chance. God said that everything produces after its kind, and has been doing that ever since Creation. That is the biblical view. You have a choice to believe whichever viewpoint sounds more reasonable to you, or whichever viewpoint seems to be confirmed by facts.

We can validate the Bible because scientists have proven it—but they will not accept that the source of life in all its variety, complexity and precision is God. They still insist it is all a chance happening—one primordial cell and chance mutations.

God said He created everything after its kind: everything! That means every human being—male and female alike.

Verses 26 and 27 tell us something more specific and remarkable about how God created mankind:

> **Then God said, "Let Us make man in Our image, according to Our likeness; let them have dominion over**

> **the fish of the sea, over the birds of the air, and over the cattle, over all the earth and over every creeping thing that creeps on the earth."**
>
> **So God created man in His own image; in the image of God He created him; male and female He created them.**

This statement is vital to our understanding of why racism is wrong—and as the next few chapters show, it is wrong from both a biblical *and* a scientific perspective.

3

In God's Image

In the Hebrew language, in which the Old Testament was originally written, the word for "image" and "likeness" found in Genesis 1:26 is *tselem.*[1] *Tselem* comes from a root word meaning "form," and, in addition to likeness and image, it implies "resemblance," or a "representative figure." This tells us that man is a copy or counterpart of God. Since God made man in His image (*tselem*), if we want to find out about man, we must first find out what God is. Then we will know what we are, because we are God's *tselem*, copy or counterpart.

In the New Testament, John chapter 4 tells us the story of Jesus going through the country of Samaria and stopping at Jacob's well outside the small town or city of Sychar. At the well, Jesus engaged in conversation with a woman who had come there to draw water. They talked about places of worship. Jesus also made the profound

---

1 James Strong, LL.D., S.T.D., "Hebrew and Aramaic Dictionary of the Old Testament," *The New Strong's Exhaustive Concordance of the Bible*, Nelson's Comfort Print ed. (Nashville: Thomas Nelson Publishers, 1995), no. 6754.

statement to her that **"...God is a Spirit, and they that worship him must worship him in spirit and in truth"** (John 4:24, KJV).

For Jesus to say that God is a Spirit, Jesus must know that God is a Spirit. How would Jesus, the Christ, the Messiah, know this? He would have to have had close proximity to God over time to be able to discern that God is a Spirit, not a physical being.

The Gospel of John begins by telling us in 1:1-2:

> **In the beginning was the Word, and the Word was with God, and the Word was God.**
>
> **He was in the beginning with God.**

Verse 2 explains that when the Bible says, **in the beginning was the Word,** the Word being referred to is a person, because it says *He* when it tells us that **He was in the beginning with God**. The rest of this Gospel makes it clear that *He* refers to the person we have come to know historically as Jesus the Christ, but Verse 2 is talking about Him in eternity past, before He took upon Himself human flesh.

Here is my point: If the Word was with God in the beginning, then the Word, which Verse 2 calls He and which the Scripture tells us is Jesus, ought to know what God is and what God is not. Jesus said, "God is a Spirit...." In Genesis 1:26, we have just seen that God said **... "Let Us make man in Our image...."** What does this tell us about Jesus? It tells us that Jesus is also a Spirit! And we know that because in Genesis 1:26, God said **... "Let Us** [plural] **make man in Our** [plural] **image...."**

God did not say, "I will make man in My image"; He said, **... "Let Us** [plural] **make man in Our** [plural] **image...."** So if we are made in the image of God, then we must be like God; we must be whatever God is. If God is a Spirit and Jesus is a Spirit and the Holy Spirit is a Spirit, and we are made in the image of God, then we must be spirits.

Let's find out more about what man is. Genesis 2:7 says:

And the LORD God formed man of the dust of the ground, and breathed into his nostrils the breath of life; and man became a living being.

This Scripture is focusing on the precise moment that God formed man into a living being. The *New King James Version* of the Bible says "being"; the traditional *King James Version* says "soul." The Bible tells us that the part of us we can see is made out of dust; in other words, it is made out of the ground. And that is no big deal. Sculptors make statues from material that comes out of the ground all the time. Even when sculptors make their statues out of iron or steel or brass or bronze, the material still comes from the ground.

Genesis says that God formed man not out of "chance mutations," but out of the dust of the ground, and breathed into his nostrils **and man became a living being.** So when God formed man out of the dust of the ground, man was not yet a man; he was just a shell in which the man that is made a copy *(tselem)* of God would live once God **breathed into his nostrils....**

Genesis 3:19 says:

"In the sweat of your face you shall eat bread till you return to the ground, for out of it you were taken; for dust you are, and to dust you shall return."

Mankind was made out of the dust of the earth. So white bodies are nothing but dust; black bodies are nothing but dust; red bodies are nothing but dust; yellow bodies are nothing but dust; and brown bodies are nothing but dust. All our bodies are nothing but piles of dust! If your beautiful furniture looks dusty, you don't stop to analyze whether it's white dust or black dust and then determine that because it's white dust, you are going to let it stay there because it's superior dust; you wipe off all the dust.

God did not put thoughts of superiority into anyone's mind. Satan did, to trick people into thinking they are something special, when in fact the skin color they are so proud of is nothing but dust. White dust, black dust, red dust, yellow dust, brown dust—just dust.

Genesis 1:26 tells us:

Then God said, "Let Us make man in Our image, according to Our likeness; let them have dominion over the fish of the sea, over the birds of the air, and over the cattle, over all the earth and over every creeping thing that creeps on the earth."

Then, in Genesis 2:7, we get the explanation of the part of us that we see, because man has a tendency to think that he and others are what we see. That is why we say "black man, red man, yellow man, white man, brown man." Yet, from the biblical perspective, what I see is not you and what you see is not me: We only see the houses in which we live; you and I actually look just like God. If God is a Spirit, then we are spirits.

In order to live in this three-dimensional physical world, we have been given a three-dimensional physical abode or body. You do not have to have a three-dimensional flesh body to be you, but you need a three-dimensional flesh body to live in this three-dimensional physical world.

Let's look again at Genesis 2:7:

And the LORD God formed man of the dust of the ground, and breathed into his nostrils the breath of life; and man became a living being.

Before God breathed into the dust house that He built, man was not; he only *became* after God breathed into him. **Breathed into his nostrils** is a symbolic statement meaning that God put the copy or counterpart of Himself inside that clay dust body, and then that dust body **became a living being** [soul].

Returning to Genesis 3:19, we read:

"In the sweat of your face [God is talking to Adam] **you shall eat bread till you return to the ground, for out of it you were taken; for dust you are, and to dust you shall return."**

Notice that the subject is not skin color; the subject is dust. God did not say you are white, you are black, you are red, you are yellow, you are brown; God said you are dust. So when you look in the mirror, say, "My body is nothing but dust. And there is no dust better than any other dust. It is all dust. And eventually it is all swept away."

First Thessalonians 5:23 tells us:

> **Now may the God of peace Himself sanctify you completely; and may your whole spirit, soul, and body be preserved blameless at the coming of our Lord Jesus Christ.**

Here we see a very clear delineation of the threefold nature of man. But notice what is conspicuously mentioned first: **your whole spirit....** God is a Spirit, and we, who are made in His image, are a *tselem*, a copy or counterpart. So if God is a Spirit, I am a spirit and you are a spirit. It's right there in the Bible: **your whole spirit, soul, and body....** We are all spirits.

Racism, especially in America, is all about color. If everyone in this nation were white, there wouldn't be any racism. If everyone in this nation were black or red or yellow or brown, there wouldn't be any racism. In our country, it's all about putting one color above the other, and in reality it all amounts to nothing but dust.

Let's look again at Genesis 2:7 (KJV):

> **And the Lord God formed man of the dust of the ground, and breathed into his nostrils the breath of life; and man became a living soul.**

The *New King James Version* of the Bible says **man became a living being....** I would like to suggest the word *creature* instead of *being*. If God created man (and Genesis 1:27 tells us: **So God created man....**), then man must be a creature. If God's creation is an individual, then each man is God's creature.

Genesis 2:7 presents another interesting aspect of this issue when it speaks of God creating the first man, Adam:

> **And the LORD God formed man of the dust of the ground, and breathed into his nostrils the breath of life; and man became a living being.**

According to *Strong's Exhaustive Concordance of the Bible,* with which most Bible students are familiar, the word *Adam* has a very interesting meaning. Keep in mind as you read this that James Strong was a Hebrew and Greek scholar, that he was white, and that for ministers and students of the Bible this concordance is as authoritative on biblical subjects as *Webster's Dictionary* is on words.

Strong says the word *Adam* literally means: "*to show blood* (in the face), i.e. *flus* or turn rosy:—be (dyed, made) red (ruddy) ... a *human being* (an individual or the species, *mankind,* etc.)."[2]

Strong says *Adam* refers to being red in the face or ruddy, not white-faced. While some have interpreted this as referring to blushing, I will show in this and in the next three chapters that Adam could not have been white, as art throughout history has portrayed him; he had to have been a man of color. You may ask, "What difference does it make?"

Let me answer that question with a question. If it does not make a difference, then why have we in America made such a huge distinction between white skin and black skin? If it does not make a difference, then my black skin should not make a difference and white skin should not make a difference—but it does, doesn't it? If it does not make any difference, then why do we have racial and color prejudice in America, primarily white against black? If it does not make a difference now, it should not have made a difference in the past; there should never have been any Whites-only drinking

---

[2] Strong, nos. 119-120.

fountains and Colored-only drinking fountains, Whites-only toilets and Colored-only toilets, and Whites-only entrances to the train and Colored-only entrances. If the color of Adam in the Bible does not make a difference, no skin color should make a difference. But as I said before, it does, doesn't it?

Recently I was watching a television special about the Bible. A famous actor was the host. During the introduction, he told us about different aspects of the upcoming show. He mentioned God, Adam and Eve, and many biblical figures. As he spoke their names, pictures flashed on the screen. One of the pictures showed God reaching His hand out to a man—and God was white. Every biblical figure, including Adam, was white—snow white!

My concern is not about what color anyone was. My concern is telling the truth rather than telling a lie. If you lie at the beginning, you place everything that follows in jeopardy; if the beginning is suspect, everything that stems from it may be held in suspicion, too. That is why many people throw out the Bible and Christianity—because they have found lies and loopholes in people's interpretations.

Why don't we just tell it as the Bible tells it instead of going by the racist traditions that Satan has caused to infiltrate the Church, traditions that make it seem as if white dust is better than colored dust?

In most Bible bookstores in the United States—I don't know about Bible bookstores in foreign countries because I haven't had the opportunity to go to them—almost all the pictures of Jesus are of a white man with light-colored hair and blue or brown eyes. At black bookstores, you will find the other extreme: Almost all the pictures of Jesus are of a black man. I don't need a black Jesus and I don't need a white Jesus; I need a real Jesus. I don't care if He had *any* color. But whatever color He was, why don't we just tell the truth about it?[3]

---

[3] A subsequent volume of *Race, Religion & Racism* will trace the genealogy of Jesus and, based on this, will suggest His true skin color.

As Christians and as the Church of the Lord Jesus Christ in the earth-realm, we should present to the world an accurate presentation of what is in the Bible, so that when other people hear what we say and investigate it in reference works, they find that it all adds up. That is why I am so concerned with truth.

In John 4:24 (KJV), Jesus said of God the Father, **"God is a Spirit."** And in Genesis 1:26, we found where God said, **"Let Us make man in Our image."** Strong's tells us that the word *Adam* also means man. Man, according to 1 Thessalonians 5:23, is a spirit, because he is a *tselem*, a copy or counterpart of God. Man is a spirit because God is a Spirit.

Man also has a soul and man lives in a clay, dust or dirt house called a body—I like to call it an earth suit—which he inhabits in order to live in this three-dimensional world.

What is the soul? We do not know exactly, but gleaning what we can from the Bible we get an idea of what is contained within it. In the soul, or soulish part of our threefold nature, is our personality. That is what makes us the unique individuals that we are. Thus, in the soul we find the desires, the will, the emotions, the mind and the human intellect.

In Greek, the body is called the *soma*. The spirit is called the *pneuma*. The spirit (*pneuma*) and the body (*soma*) can be separated.[4] That is what death is: the departure of the spirit and the soul from the body, the *pneuma* being separated from the *soma*. But the spirit (*pneuma*) and the soul (*psuche*) can only be distinguished; that is, we can make a distinction between them, but they cannot be parted from each other.

---

[4] James Strong, LL.D., S.T.D., "Greek Dictionary of the New Testament," *The New Strong's Exhaustive Concordance of the Bible*, Nelson's Comfort Print ed. (Nashville: Thomas Nelson Publishers, 1995), nos. 4983, 4151 and 5590.

I like to think of it this way: the spirit (*pneuma*) and the soul (*psuche*) are like wetness and water, they go hand in hand. You can't remove wetness from water; if you get water, you get wetness; if you get the spirit (*pneuma*) you get the soul (*psuche*). But I can separate the spirit and the soul from the body, just as I can separate the water and the wetness from a glass. The glass represents the body or the *soma*; the water and its wetness represent the spirit and the soul or the *pneuma* and the *psuche*.

Based on the account in Genesis, and on scientific information, both of which we will look at in chapters four, five and six, I believe that Adam had to be a man of color. He could not have been what we call European white. Our traditional concept of God, the Bible, Jesus and the apostles has been Eurocentric. Some Blacks have been so bewildered by this Eurocentric concept that they have become Afrocentric. I don't subscribe to either point of view. I subscribe to the Christocentric concept. I am not going to make Adam or Jesus white and I am not going to make them black. Why not let them be who they are? Why do they have to be white? Why do they have to be black?

Historically, the art that depicts biblical themes has been from a Eurocentric point of view. The question is, is this a biblically, historically and scientifically accurate portrayal of mankind as created by the God of the Bible? To answer this, it is necessary for us to see what the Bible, historians, biologists and anthropologists have said about this subject, to bring out information that, in part, has been hidden from people's general knowledge.

An untruth was promulgated many years ago to make it look as if God is white. That sent a false message to white people and to people of color around the world. It has contributed to Whites feeling superior and others feeling inferior. That is not the biblical perspective at all.

The business of slavery in America was oppression and degradation of the black race, fostered by the idea of white supremacy—which itself stems from the concept that God is white, Adam was white, Abraham was white, Jesus was white and everyone else of any significance in the Bible was white. White is right, and anything that is not white is not quite right. This lie gave the justification to enslave and put down people who were not white. And it is antithetical to what the Bible tells us.

Before I go into the Bible's perspective in more depth in the next chapter, I would like first to present some relevant scriptural background.

Titus 3:9 says:

But avoid foolish disputes, genealogies, contentions, and strivings about the law; for they are unprofitable and useless.

First Timothy 1:4 tells us:

nor give heed to fables and endless genealogies, which cause disputes rather than godly edification which is in faith.

People who do not understand my position are going to use these two verses to accuse me of starting strife and causing division in the Body of Christ. But when they accuse me of that, they will be doing it out of ignorance of the Word of God. Let me explain: I have a method of reading the Bible that I call the flip-flop method: What I like to do is flip the Scripture over and read what it does *not* say; this helps me to dramatize or magnify what it does say. Let's look again at 1 Timothy 1:4:

nor give heed to fables and endless genealogies....

Notice what it does not say: It does not say "nor give heed to genealogies"; it says, **nor give heed to endless genealogies....** I am not going to present *endless* genealogies, I am going to present genealogies that have an end.

Again, Titus 3:9 says:

… avoid foolish … genealogies….

It does not say to "avoid genealogies," it says to **avoid foolish … genealogies.** The Bible is telling us to avoid foolish disputes, foolish contentions, foolish strivings, because they are unprofitable and useless.

In the next chapter, I am not going to be dealing with foolish genealogies; I am going to be dealing with genealogies that have a definite purpose. And in doing so, I am right in line with the Word of God.

4

One Blood, One Flesh, All Nations

After the great flood, seventy-one distinct nations descended from Noah's three sons. Although we hear of the black, white, red, yellow and brown races, there are really only three races, because Noah only had three sons: Shem, Ham and Japheth. The three of them were commanded by God to go forth and repopulate the earth, and from them the nations of the earth were established. They are the patriarchs of the three major color groups that exist today.

From Ham, the father of the so-called black color group, came a total of thirty separate nations.

God Almighty, Who knows the future, would have known the problems that would arise as a result of creating a variety of skin colors. It seems that He could have made everything a lot easier by making everybody one color. But we have many colors, and they all came from the same source, so He must have had a purpose in creating them. We need to think about that purpose, and we need to see how we fit into it.

Actually, He really did create only one color—but we will discuss that later.

For now, let's look at what Genesis 10:6-20 tells us about the nations that came from Ham:

> **The sons of Ham were Cush, Mizraim, Put, and Canaan.**
>
> **The sons of Cush were Seba, Havilah, Sabtah, Raamah, and Sabtechah; and the sons of Raamah were Sheba and Dedan.**
>
> **Cush begot Nimrod; he began to be a mighty one on the earth.**
>
> **He was a mighty hunter before the Lord; therefore it is said, "Like Nimrod the mighty hunter before the Lord."**
>
> **And the beginning of his kingdom was Babel, Erech, Accad, and Calneh, in the land of Shinar.**
>
> **From that land he went to Assyria and built Nineveh, Rehoboth Ir, Calah,**
>
> **and Resen between Nineveh and Calah (that is the principal city).**
>
> **Mizraim begot Ludim, Anamim, Lehabim, Naphtuhim,**
>
> **Pathrusim, and Casluhim (from whom came the Philistines and Caphtorim).**
>
> **Canaan begot Sidon his first-born, and Heth**
>
> **the Jebusite, the Amorite, and the Girgashite,**
>
> **the Hivite, the Arkite, and the Sinite;**
>
> **the Arvadite, the Zemarite, and the Hamathite. Afterward the families of the Canaanites were dispersed.**

> **And the border of the Canaanites was from Sidon as you go toward Gerar, as far as Gaza; then as you go toward Sodom, Gomorrah, Admah, and Zeboiim, as far as Lasha.**
>
> **These were the sons of Ham, according to their families, according to their languages, in their lands and in their nations.**

In years gone by, when I would read the Bible, especially Genesis, and read all these names, it would seem very boring. But in reality, all of this is relevant to us today. In a future volume of *Race, Religion & Racism*, we will go through the genealogy of Jesus Christ Himself. We will go all the way back to Adam through some of the people named here, and we will find out the truth about where we came from, why we are, and what we ought to be. When we do this, everything will fit into place like the pieces of a jigsaw puzzle which, once put together, form a beautiful picture.

From Shem, the father of the Semitic or yellow color group, which includes Jews, Arabs, Middle-Eastern and Asiatic people, came a total of twenty-seven separate nations. As Genesis 10:21-31 explains:

> **And children were born also to Shem, the father of all the children of Eber, the brother of Japheth the elder.**
>
> **The sons of Shem were Elam, Asshur, Arphaxad, Lud, and Aram.**
>
> **The sons of Aram were Uz, Hul, Gether, and Mash.**
>
> **Arphaxad begot Salah, and Salah begot Eber.**
>
> **To Eber were born two sons: the name of one was Peleg, for in his days the earth was divided; and his brother's name was Joktan.**
>
> **Joktan begot Almodad, Sheleph, Hazarmaveth, Jerah,**

> **Hadoram, Uzal, Diklah,**
>
> **Obal, Abimael, Sheba,**
>
> **Ophir, Havilah, and Jobab. All these were the sons of Joktan.**
>
> **And their dwelling place was from Mesha as you go toward Sephar, the mountain of the east.**
>
> **These were the sons of Shem, according to their families, according to their languages, in their lands, according to their nations.**

From Japheth, the father of the white or Caucasian color group, which includes the Germanic peoples of northern Europe, came a total of fifteen separate nations. As Genesis 10:2-5 says:

> **The sons of Japheth were Gomer, Magog, Madai, Javan, Tubal, Meshech, and Tiras.**
>
> **The sons of Gomer were Ashkenaz, Riphath, and Togarmah.**
>
> **The sons of Javan were Elishah, Tarshish, Kittim, and Dodanim.**
>
> **From these the coastland peoples of the Gentiles were separated into their lands, everyone according to his language, according to their families, into their nations.**

Genesis 10:32 tells us:

> **These were the families of the sons of Noah, according to their generations, in their nations; and from these the nations were divided on the earth after the flood**

So everyone on our planet—every color group that exists today—came from Shem, Ham and Japheth. The reason there are five color groups now instead of three is that there has been so much mixing throughout history. Most people on the planet are mixed; every one of us is descended from Noah's three sons, and the majority are dark-complexioned, not light-complexioned.

In *Strong's Concordance*, we find a definition of the word *nation* because the words *race* and *ethnic* as we know them, referring to different color groups, are not found in the Bible. The word for *nation* in the original Greek is *ethnos,* which *Strong's* says means "a *race* (as of the same *habitat*), [in other words, living in the same geographical area]; i.e. a *tribe*; spec. a *foreign* (*non-Jewish*) one (usually by impl. *pagan*): —Gentile, heathen, nation, people."[1]

Acts 17:26 says:

> **"And He has made from one blood every nation of men to dwell on all the face of the earth...."**

Notice this: **... one blood every nation....** Every nation comes out of one blood. That is why I said earlier that there is only one color—and I am going to show you this scientifically in chapter 6. There is only one color; what we see in people is a myriad of colors created by a continual mixing of color groups.

First Corinthians 15:39 gives us further confirmation:

> **All flesh is not the same flesh, but there is one kind of flesh of men, another flesh of animals, another of fish, and another of birds.**

All flesh of men is the same; it is the flesh of mankind. When Paul says, "All flesh is not the same flesh," he means man's flesh is not the same as the flesh of fish, birds and animals, but that all men

---

[1] James Strong, LL.D., S.T.D., "Greek Dictionary of the New Testament," *The New Strong's Exhaustive Concordance of the Bible*, Nelson's Comfort Print ed. (Nashville: Thomas Nelson Publishers, 1995), no. 1484.

are of one flesh. As much as some, perhaps, would like to deny it, this black flesh of mine is the same as white, yellow, brown or red flesh, regardless of what color my flesh may appear to be.

We derive our English word *ethnic* from *ethnos,* and we talk about different ethnic groups. But there is only one group. God has told us this in so many ways, and we still refuse to listen; we would rather listen to the devil and make arbitrary distinctions, which really are not distinctions at all. They are only foul smells in the nostrils of God. Because He said **... one blood every nation ...** and **... one kind of flesh of me ....** *All men's flesh is th same.*

I am almost reluctant to quote Romans 12:3, because it is such an indictment of the historical Church of the Lord Jesus Christ. But it is important for us to comprehend the vastness of the difference between what the Bible says and how people—people who call themselves Christians—have acted.

Keep in mind that when we read these New Testament Scriptures, it is God the Father talking to His blood-bought, blood-washed, redeemed children. That means He is talking to everyone who claims Jesus as Savior and Lord, be they black, white, red, brown or yellow.

In Romans 12:3, Paul directed his letter to the Church at Rome. That is because the Church in America did not yet exist. God wanted to get His Word into the earth-realm, so that when the Church in America was established, people here could also apply God's Word for themselves, even though it was originally given to the Romans.

> **For I say, through the grace given to me, to everyone who is among you, not to think of himself more highly than he ought to think....**

What is God saying here? He is telling us, as Christians, that we are not supposed to think more highly of ourselves than we ought to think. The whole existence of racism in America shows us that too many white people are apparently thinking more highly of themselves than they ought to think, when, in fact, they are nothing but dust.

Because some Whites have thought more highly of themselves than they should have, they have planted the monster of racial inferiority into the minds of others who did not look like them. By treating the minorities as inferior, they have conveyed the idea that minorities are not as good as the white majority. Consequently, Blacks and others have thought less of themselves than they should have. But in reality, they are the same flesh as the ones who think so highly of themselves.

How many bloods? One. How many nations from that blood? All. How many different kinds of flesh? One. And one is no better than the other.

That is why racism is a terrible travesty of justice.

Let's look at Romans 12:3-5 in more detail:

> **For I say, through the grace given to me, to everyone who is among you, not to think of himself more highly than he ought to think, but to think soberly, as God has dealt to each one a measure of faith.**
>
> **For as we have many members in one body, but all the members do not have the same function,**
>
> **so we, being many, are one body in Christ, and individually members of one another.**

Note what this says: **... one body in Christ, and individually members of one another....** We are in the same body, so we should have the same care for one another; as far as God is concerned, we are one. This means that something is radically wrong in the Church, and has been since the black man first stepped on the American shore in chains.

If we are members of one another and we claim to be in the Church, and we claim to be Christians, then as black as I am and as white or red or brown or yellow as you are, we are one. That is what the Bible says. Racism has been allowed to exist—to thrive—and lies have been passed on from generation to generation to generation, because people have not been reading the Bible.

Again, Romans 12:5 tells us:

so we, being many, are one body in Christ....

This means that everyone who claims to be a Christian is one with everyone else who claims to be a Christian. This is emphasized in the next part of the Scripture:

... and individually members of one another.

If we are members of one another, how can part of us be inferior and the other part be superior?

Not only are the lies of racism in direct opposition to the teachings of the Bible, the next chapters show that they also go against the latest findings of science about the genetic composition of the human race.

5

Africa, the Birthplace of Humanity

Where did the human race begin geographically? Genesis 2:7-10 tells us:

And the LORD God formed man of the dust of the ground, and breathed into his nostrils the breath of life; and man became a living being [or, as the traditional *King James* says, a living soul].

The LORD God planted a garden eastward in Eden, and there He put the man whom He had formed.

And out of the ground the LORD God made every tree grow that is pleasant to the sight and good for food. The tree of life was also in the midst of the garden, and the tree of the knowledge of good and evil.

Now a river went out of Eden to water the garden....

The Scripture does not say the river went out of the *garden* of Eden; it says the river went out of *Eden*. Therefore we know that Eden was a geographical area larger than the garden that was in it; it also tells us that Eden was the source of a river.

Let's look at Verse 11:

The name of the first is Pishon; it is the one which skirts the whole land of Havilah, where there is gold.

This tells us that the first river, Pishon, ran along the outside edge of Havilah. Reviewing Verse 11 and continuing through Verse 13, we learn:

The name of the first is Pishon; it is the one which skirts the whole land of Havilah, where there is gold.

And the gold of that land is good. Bdellium and the onyx stone are there.

The name of the second river is Gihon; it is the one which goes around the whole land of Cush.

I want to note the word *Cush:* In the traditional *King James*, the word *Cush* is translated as "Ethiopia." So we know that the land of Cush is today called Ethiopia.

Verses 14 and 15 go on to say:

The name of the third river is Hiddekel; it is the one which goes toward the east of Assyria. The fourth river is the Euphrates.

Then the LORD God took the man and put him in the garden of Eden to tend and keep it.

Adam is not to keep Eden, but the garden of Eden. It is interesting that in describing the garden of Eden, the names Havilah and Cush (Ethiopia) are mentioned.

Havilah was a son of Cush, who was a son of Ham. Since Ham was black, Cush had to be black and Cush's son Havilah also had to be black. It is not my contention that everyone in the Bible was black. However, in all fairness to the facts stated in the Bible—which contradict what the white church and society have been saying, that everyone was white—it's clear that some people were black. Among them were Ham, Cush and Havilah.

Liars have said that Ham was cursed with blackness. Slave owners said that black skin was a curse. But the Scriptures never say that black skin is a curse.[1] In fact, the garden of Eden was in a land that the Bible associates with black people: Cush and Havilah. Indeed, since the time of Ham, this land was populated by Blacks. It had to be, since Ethiopia (the land of Cush) is located on the continent of Africa—not Europe.

One of Ham's other sons was Mizraim and the word *Mizraim* in the Hebrew language translates to the English word *Egypt*. So if Ham was black and his son Mizraim was black, and Mizraim means *Egypt*, then the people of Egypt also must have been black, regardless of the lies in the movie *The Ten Commandments*, which depicts Pharaoh as white. I don't care what he was, but I do care if someone tells me he was something that he was not, and then uses that false information against me to keep black people enslaved.

Where is Egypt located? Of course it is on the continent of Africa. And even today it is still populated mostly by dark-skinned people, not by Caucasians.

So we know from a biblical perspective that the garden of Eden was in Ethiopia, on what later became known as the black continent of Africa, and that the Egyptians—also Africans—were black. What does science say about where the human race started and about what color the first human beings were?

According to a 1988 article entitled, "The Search for Adam and Eve," in *Newsweek* magazine:

> The scientists' Eve–subject of one of the most provocative anthropological theories in a decade–was more likely

---

[1] The so-called curse of Ham will be discussed further in Chapter 7 and will also be addressed in a subsequent volume.

> a dark-haired, black-skinned woman, roaming a hot savanna in search of food.
>
> ... Most evidence so far indicates that Eve lived in sub-Saharan Africa.
>
> ... [Scientists] think our common ancestor must have lived ... at least a million years ago, because that was when humans first left Africa and began spreading out over the world....[2]

In this same article, noted Harvard paleontologist Steven J. Gould is quoted as saying:

> It makes us realize that all human beings, despite differences in external appearance, are really members of a single entity that's had a very recent origin in one place. There is a kind of biological brotherhood that's much more profound than we ever realized.[3]

Gould is not presenting his material from the context of the Scriptures; he is doing it as a scientist, yet he is telling us that we have a common brotherhood. God has been trying to tell us this since the beginning of time and, unfortunately, few people in the Church have been listening.

In *Sex and Race,* historian J.A. Rogers quotes from *Key to Culture*, in which Joseph McCabe says:

> "Primitive man, let us remember, was a colored man, a dusky person.... Four thousand years ago, when civilization was already one or two thousand years old, white men were just a bunch of semi-savages on the outskirts of the civilized world. If there had been anthropologists

---

2 John Tierney, Lynda Wright and Karen Springen, "The Search for Adam and Eve," *Newsweek*, v. CXI, no. 2 (January 11, 1988), 46-47.

3 Tierney, Wright, Springen, 47.

> in Crete, Egypt, and Babylonia, they would have pronounced the white race obviously inferior, and might have discoursed learnedly on the superior germ-plasm or glands of colored folk."[4]

In the same book, Rogers asks this provocative question, "Were the Jews originally Negroes?"[5] Rogers bases his question on the fact that "only seventy Jews went to Egypt, but according to the Bible, 600,000 men left it, which must have meant an additional two or three million women and children. Since the Jews were slaves their women were undoubtedly concubines of the Egyptians...."[6]

This situation parallels the situation in America thousands of years later when black women were concubines of the white slave masters and slave owners. As we all know, two black people cannot produce a mulatto; two black people cannot produce a quadroon; and two black people cannot produce an octoroon.[7] It takes some white in the mix somewhere. And there was no way that the black slave could go into Massa's house and take Massa's daughter—Massa had to go out to the slave quarters and take the slave's daughter. That is where these shades of color originated in

---

[4] J.A. Rogers, *Sex and Race: Negro-Caucasian Mixing in All Ages and All Lands*, 9th ed., v. 1 (St. Petersburg, Florida: Helga M. Rogers, 1967), 50.

[5] Rogers, 91.

[6] Rogers, 91.

[7] Personally, I don't use the terms *mulatto, quadroon* or *octoroon*. I am using them now as I used the terms *house nigger, field nigger* and *nigger*—which I also personally never use—because they have been used in print and in movies, and because they are used by some people in everyday conversation. I am simply being real; I don't mean to hurt anyone with these words. And if they are hurtful, we must reflect on the fact that it is because they are so tinged with the lies of racism.

our country. In Africa, you won't find among Africans the light-skinned black people we have in America.

Let's look again at what Rogers is saying:

> Since the Jews were slaves their women were undoubtedly concubines of the Egyptians and must have produced mixed offspring. After more than three centuries of slavery almost every trace of the first seventy Jews must have been lost, together with their culture.[8]

This sounds like what happened to black people in America, doesn't it? Rogers says that during the time of their enslavement, Jewish culture became Egyptian culture.

> To get an idea of what must have happened to only those seventy Jews, think of what has happened to Negroes in the United States who came in hundreds of thousands over a period of centuries and not all at once as the Jews did in Egypt. The Negroes are so Americanized that were it not for their color one would forget that they ever came from Africa.
> The falashas, or Black Jews of Ethiopia, are probably very ancient. They claim lineal descent from Abraham, Isaac and Jacob, call themselves Beta-Israel (The Chosen People), and observe the passover. [9]

Rogers also informs us:

> Increasingly it is being said in the most informed scientific circles that the Negro was the ancestor of the human race. Henry Fairfield Osborn, the late head of the American Museum of Natural History, who had himself a strong tinge of white fanaticism, said, "Ne-

---

[8] Rogers, 91.
[9] Rogers, 91-92.

> groid stock is even more ancient than Caucasian or Mongolian man."[10]

Rogers quotes René Verneau, head of the Paleontological Institute of Paris, as saying, "Recent discoveries seem to indicate that the Negro element preceded the White and the Yellow everywhere."[11] Geologist Griffith Taylor, Rogers reports, similarly concludes, "A major principle of ecology tells us that the Negrito was … the earliest to develop of the five races."[12] Taylor goes on to say that "the Negritos, or little Negroes, were the first in Europe, after the Neanderthal, a near-human Negroid type, and that the Negritos 'introduced' their culture 'all over the world.' The original color of primitive man was 'black.' "[13]

These facts were known for years, but they weren't taught to any of us, black or white. That's why many of us still find them so surprising.

Regarding one of the black civilizations that evolved thousands of years later, the Greek historian Herodotus, who lived 500 years before Christ and was known as the Father of History, tells us:

> There can be no doubt that the Colchians [the inhabitants of Colchia, an ancient province of Asia, east of the Black Sea] are an Egyptian race. Before I heard any mention of the fact from others, I had remarked it myself. After the thought had struck me, I made inquiries on the subject both in Colchia and in Egypt, and I found that the Colchians had a more distinct recollection of the Egyptians, than the Egyptians had of them.
>
> Still the Egyptians said that they believed the Colchians to be descended from the army of Sesostris. My own

---

[10] Rogers, 28.

[11] Rogers, 28.

[12] Rogers, 28.

[13] Rogers, 28.

> conjectures were founded, first, on the fact that they are black skinned and have woolly hair; which certainly amounts to but little, since several other nations are so too; but further and more especially, on the circumstance that the Colchians, the Egyptians and the Ethiopians, are the only nations who have practiced circumcision from the earliest times. The Phoenicians and the Syrians of Palestine themselves confess that they learnt the custom of the Egyptians; and the Syrians who dwell about the rivers Thermodon and Parthenius, as well as their neighbors the Macronians, say that they have recently adopted it from the Colchians. Now these are the only nations who use circumcision, and it is plain that they all imitate herein the Egyptians. With respect to the Ethiopians, indeed, I cannot decide whether they learnt the practice of the Egyptians, or the Egyptians of them—it is undoubtedly of very ancient date in Ethiopia—but that the others derived their knowledge of it from Egypt is clear to me, from the fact that the Phoenicians, when they come to have commerce with the Greeks, cease to follow the Egyptians in this custom and allowed their children to remain uncircumcised. I will add a further proof of the identity of the Egyptians and the Colchians. These two nations weave their linen in exactly the same way, and this is a way entirely unknown to the rest of the world; they also in their whole mode of life and in their language resemble one another. The Colchians' linen is called by the Greeks, Sardonian, while that which comes from Egypt is known as Egyptian.[14]

Clearly, the ancients knew that the civilizations of Egypt and Colchia were black. Indeed, J. A. Rogers points out that "Aristotle

---

[14] Francis R.B. Godolphin, ed., George Rawlinson, trans., Persian Wars, Book 2, *The Greek Historians: The Complete and Unabridged Historical Works of Herodotus, Thucydides, Xenophon, and Arrian* (New York: Random House, 1942), 130-131.

in his 'Physiognomy,' Chapter VI, distinctly mentions the Ethiopians as having woolly hair and the Egyptians as being black-skinned."[15] Yet as I've noted, in every movie we see about Egypt, Pharaoh is white; the only time we see a Black is when he is a slave.

Rogers goes on to say that according to Count M.C. de Volney, author of *The Ruins of Empire*, "The ancient Egyptians were real Negroes of the same species as the other present natives of Africa,"[16] and that "to the race of Negroes ... the object of our extreme contempt ... we owe our arts, sciences and even the very use of speech!"[17]

Again, these are facts they did not teach us in school. The only thing we were taught was that Blacks came to America on slave ships and picked cotton. Obviously, as we have seen in this chapter, there is a great deal more to say. And as we will see in the next chapter, science has discovered facts about the history and heritage of Blacks that need to be taught not just in schools, but in churches.

---

[15] J.A. Rogers, *From "Superman" to Man* (St. Petersburg, Florida: Helga M. Rogers, 1968; reprint 1989), 18 (page citations are to the reprint edition).

[16] Rogers, 18.

[17] Rogers, 19.

6

Adam, Eve and Genetics

As we discussed in Part One, since 1619, when the first Africans were taken off a Dutch ship and slavery officially began in America, there has been a concerted effort on the part of the Church and society to make it appear that black people are subhuman, and therefore it was all right first to enslave them, and then, on freeing them, to treat them as second-class citizens.

This has given Whites the idea that they have an inalienable right to look down on people of color. What in the world have black people done in human history to deserve such treatment? There is only one answer: being born black. I am not ignoring the idol worship of Egypt and Ethiopia, and the biblical prophecies concerning God's judgment on them; Egypt and Ethiopia were the leading nations of the world at one time, and it was prophesied that they would fall from their position of prominence because of their sin.

Some have said that black people in America have suffered as we have because of the sins of our forefathers. I take issue with that proposition and here is why: God, our heavenly Father, is consistent. He does not change. Malachi 3:6 says, **"For I am the Lord, I do not change...."** Neither is He a respecter of persons. Ethiopians, as far as I can determine, from a biblical perspective, were never considered the chosen people, the people through whom God would reveal

Himself to the world. I cannot believe, nor have I found any biblical evidence to support the contention, that God would treat Egypt and Ethiopia any differently because of the sin of idol worship than He would treat Israel for committing the same sin. God said to Israel that the children would be visited with the iniquity of their fathers—but, as far as I can tell, not forever.

Numbers 14:18 says:

> **"The Lord is longsuffering and abundant in mercy, forgiving iniquity and transgression; but He by no means clears the guilty, visiting the iniquity of the fathers on the children to the third and fourth generation."**

So the Bible specifies **"the third and fourth generation,"** not a thousand generations! Exodus 20:5 says almost the same thing, again specifying the third and fourth generation.

We must also take into consideration that at the time of their greatest power and influence, when they were punished for idol worship, Egypt and Ethiopia were not considered Christian nations. Further, nowhere in the Scriptures, at least to my knowledge, has God ever used a Christian nation such as America to chastise or punish a heathen nation such as Egypt or Ethiopia. Moreover, God has never used the Bible, as has been done in America, to punish an ethnic group, such as the black race.

The whole issue, once again, is the exterior of our flesh bodies: the color of our skin. From a psychological point of view, if you have been told all your life in various ways, sometimes directly, sometimes subliminally, that you are superior, it is bound to make you feel good about yourself. And when you have been told that some other people are inferior, you are going to have negative feelings toward them. And when the other people have been told all their lives—through art, through popular culture, through preaching from pulpits, through virtually every message that their nation has sent to them over the years—that they are inferior, they are not going to feel good about themselves. They are going to have low self-esteem.

As a man of color, as a minister of the Gospel and as a Christian, I am not concerned about trying to prove that God and all of His angels were black so that I can feel good about myself. I really do not care what color God or His angels are, or what color anyone else is for that matter; what I care about is truth. Lies upset me; they stir my righteous indignation, because when you lie to me, you are telling me you have something to hide. If you had nothing to hide, you could tell me the truth. And perhaps what you are trying to hide is your own inferiority by clouding it in an apparent superiority and transferring your inferiority onto someone else.

Religion in America is the thing that has kept racism, racial prejudice and color prejudice at the level that it is. The Church has been responsible, and that is what I have been assigned to address.

I've stated it before and I will state it again: Slavery could never have existed in America without the consent of the Church. When you bring God into the picture and justify the treatment of black people based on the idea that God says they are inferior and you are superior, that gives great credibility to what you are saying.[1] If God said that black people are inferior, they would have to be inferior, because God said it. But God did not say that; those who supposedly were representing God said it, but God never said it. In fact, God says the opposite.

A recent article in *The Washington Post* gives us additional evidence about the geographical and biological beginnings of mankind and the artificiality of what we think of as the distinctions between the races:

> The overwhelming conclusion of anthropologists, in short, is that no physical feature distinguishes any race. Not even a combination of traits will do the job.

---

[1] In a subsequent volume of *Race, Religion & Racism*, I will discuss in more detail the ways in which religion has been used to foster racism in America.

> We all descended from black people. Because humans evolved in Africa, the first people probably had dark skin. The white people of Europe descended from Africans who migrated north, between 100,000 and 200,000 years ago, and lost their coloring.[2]

When I talked about Adam and Eve, I pointed out that the Bible plainly tells us the garden of Eden was located on the continent we have come to know as Africa. Here, I am not referring to the work of Christians or theologians, but of scientists, and the scientists are more in line with the Bible than so-called Christians are.

It is because Christians try to make everything and everyone white that I have to raise the question, why tell a lie and then perpetuate it? It has to be a lie, because we only have one record of creation, and it goes from Adam through the Old Covenant all the way to Jesus.

Racists will go to any lengths to prove that black people are inferior and white people are superior. They go so far as to make it appear as though the original people God created were white, and there was another creation for all the other people in the world. But that is impossible; Adam and Eve could not have been white. There is no record anywhere in the world, past or present, of two white people giving birth to a black baby. It won't work genetically. There is only one combination that can produce black and white, and we will examine that later in this chapter.

First, let's look at what genetic research tells us about where the human race started:

> A new analysis of a type of human gene supports the theory that humanity started in Africa and did not evolve simultaneously in Europe and Asia, scientists said....

---

[2] Boyce Rensberger, "Forget the Old Labels. Here's a New Way to Look at Race," Horizons: The Learning Section, *Washington Post*, no. 346 (Wednesday, November 16, 1994), H01-H7.

> Two African groups, the Pygmies in central Africa and the Kung in southern Africa, may be the most "direct" descendants of those early humans, said Linda Vigilant, a genetics specialist at the University of California in Berkeley.[3]

Time magazine tells us that a color map of world genetic variation by geneticists Luca Cavalli-Sforza, Paolo Menozzi and Albert Piazza, the fossil record and other physical evidence indicate "that Africa was the birthplace of humanity and thus the starting point of the original human migrations."[4]

Again, these are not preachers taking text from the Bible, they are scientists, and they are saying everything that the Bible says without saying the Bible said it. It's confirmation; God is confirming His Word by secular science! And that is awesome information: Everyone came from Africa, and the Bible said so. But now scientists are saying it too.

There is really only one race, the human race. That is what the Bible tells us in Acts 17:26: That God made all nations out of one blood. The Bible also tells us in 1 Corinthians 15:39 that there is one kind of flesh of man. The Bible never distinguishes by skin color or appearance, but only by kindred, tongue, people and nation. *Never* by color. But I am sorry to say that the white church uses color as a designation.

We cannot deny the fact that there are people who have certain features such as skin color in common. But the human races are all part of one species—Homo sapiens, or wise men.[5] That tells us that

---

[3] Robert Engelman, "Geneticist: We're All From Africa," Science & Technology, *Scripps Howard News Service*.

[4] Sribala Subramanian, "The Story in Our Genes," Science Section, *Time*, Domestic ed., v. 145, no. 2 (January 16, 1995), 54-55.

[5] Homo sapiens is from *Homo*, meaning genus or name and sapiens, which is derived from Latin, meaning wise, intelligent. See *Merriam Webster's Collegiate Dictionary*, 10th ed. (Springfield, Massachusetts: Merriam-Webster, Inc., 1993), 556.

all colors, or races, can freely interbreed and produce offspring. If not, each race would have to be classified as a separate species. But as scientists have informed us, there is very little biological difference between races or colors.

The religionists, the white supremacists and the slave masters tried to tell us through the years that the white race is pure. Yet modern science contradicts the idea that there were ever pure races.

> Until the mid-20th century, most researchers assumed that so-called pure races once existed. Those early thinkers had great trouble figuring out who belonged in which race and decided that was simply because migrations and intermarriage had mixed up, or blended, the once-distinct traits. Today, most anthropologists hold that pure races never existed. They think that human beings have always been migrating and intermarrying, spreading new genes worldwide.[6]

The root of racism in America is the issue of superiority/inferiority based on color. Until that lie is exposed and we realize that God created us from one blood and there is only one kind of flesh of man, we are going to miss the mark.

I hold the white Christian church in America responsible for racial and color prejudice in the Church. Black people and Hispanics were not the ones who left the inner cities and moved to the suburbs. I hear Jesus say **go ye into**—not *away from* but *into*—**all the world...** (Mark 16:15, KJV). Is the white church saying that the ghettos, the inner cities, are not part of the world? The white church, part of the Body of Christ in America, has all the resources, controls the wealth, has the power, and yet it ran off and left the inner cities. Then the white church has the audacity to criticize people in the ghetto for acting like animals, when white society has treated black people like animals for almost 400 years. If some black people have acted like

---

[6] Rensberger, H01-H7.

aimals, so have some white people—and the white people have not been subjected to 400 years of prejudice.

Our country is in turmoil. It is in dire trouble. And it is because we have been practicing religion instead of Christianity. There is a big difference between the two.

Let's see what else science has to tell us about skin color. Ken Ham, Andrew Snelling and Karl Wieland, authors of *The Answers Book,* are creation scientists, with degrees in biology, geology, and medicine, respectively. They deal with the question of skin color in a clear, concise way. Even without any background in science, you will be able to understand their presentation.

As *The Answers Book* explains:

> It is easy to think that since different groups of people have yellow skin, red skin, black skin, white skin, and brown skin, there must be many different skin pigments or colorings....
>
> The fact is, however, that there is only one skin color: melanin. This is a brownish pigment which we all have in special cells in our skin.... If we produce only a little melanin, it means that we will be European white. If our skin produces a great deal of melanin, we will be a very deep black. And in between, of course, are all shades of brown.[7]

The Answers Book continues:

> We also need to be aware that one is not born with a genetically fixed amount of melanin, but rather with a genetically fixed potential to produce a certain amount in response to sunlight. For example, if you are a Caucasian, you may have noticed that when your friends headed for

---

[7] Ken Ham, Andrew Snelling and Karl Wieland, *The Answers Book: Answers to the 12 Most-Asked Questions on Genesis and Creation/Evolution,* Revised ed. (Green Forest, Arizona: Master Books, 1990), 133-134.

> the beach at the very beginning of summer, they may, if they spent all their time indoors during the winter, have all been more or less the same pale white. As the summer went on, however, some became much darker than others. Even very dark-skinned races are not born with such a skin color. It takes exposure to sunlight to switch on the melanin factories in the skin. In very dark-skinned people, the areas such as the palms of the hands and the soles of the feet, which are very rarely exposed to sunlight, generally stay much lighter than the rest of the body.
>
> Let's look at a few observations which can help us to explain how many different skin colors can arise in a short time. (From here on, whenever we use such words as "different colors," we are, strictly speaking, referring to different shades of the one color). If a person from a very black race marries someone from a very white race, their offspring (called mulattos) are mid-brown. It has long been known that if people of mulatto descent marry, their offspring may be virtually any color, ranging from very black to very white.[8]

My wife's family is a perfect example of this. My wife's mother's grandfather was a white man, and my wife's mother was as fair as any white person. Her husband on the other hand was black skinned and very dark. They had thirteen children. Eleven of the children were slightly different shades of medium brown. One child was almost white and one almost black. Thus, my wife and her brothers and sisters have the variety of skin colors that come from having at least one parent whose own parentage is mixed.

The Answers Book tells us:

> Understanding this gives us the clues we need for our overall question, so we must first look, in a simple way, at some of the basic facts of heredity.

---

[8] Ham, Snelling and Wieland, 135.

Each of us carries in our body information which describes us in the way a blueprint describes a finished building. It determines not only that we will be human beings, rather than cabbages or crocodiles, but also whether we will have blue eyes, short nose, long legs, etc. When a male sperm fertilizes an egg, all the information that specifies how the person will be built (ignoring such superimposed factors as exercise and diet) is already present.

... The human blueprint is written in a code (or language convention) which is carried on a very long chemical called DNA.

The word "gene" means a small part of that information which carries the instructions for only one feature....

[The fertilized egg]—where does all its information, its genes, come from? One half has come from the father (carried by the sperm), and the other half from the mother (carried in the egg). Genes come in matching pairs....[9]

We know that skin color is governed by at least two (possibly more) sets of genes. Let's call them A and B, with the correspondingly more silent genes, a and b.... (The small letters in this case code for a small amount of melanin.) So a very dark race which, on intermarriage, kept producing only very dark offspring, would be AA BB; the same situation for a very fair-skinned race would be aa bb. Let's look at what combinations would result in a mulatto (the offspring of an AA BB and aa bb union).

What would happen ... if two such mid-brown mulatto people were to marry?

Surprisingly, we find that an entire range of color, from very white to very black, can result in only one

[9] Ham, Snelling and Wieland, 135-137.

> generation, beginning with this particular type of mid-brown parents.
>
> Those children born with AA BB, who are pure black (in the sense of consistently having no other types of offspring), have no genes for lightness at all. If they were to marry and migrate to a place where their offspring could not intermarry with people of different colors, all their children will be black—a pure "black line" will result. Those who are aa bb are white; if they marry other whites and migrate to a place where their offspring cannot marry other colors, a pure (in the same sense) "white line" will result—they have lost the genes which give them the ability to be black, that is, to produce a large amount of melanin.[10]

Now you can understand why Adam and Eve could not have been white. If they had been white, they would have had no genes for any color other than white. They would only have produced white children, just as Blacks can only produce black children. You have to have a combination of genes for both black and white to do otherwise. As the *The Answers Book* puts it:

> So you can see how it is easily possible, beginning with two middle-brown parents, to get not only all the colors, but also races with permanently different shades of coloring.[11]

Thus, Adam and Eve could not have been black or white but had to be mid-brown—because only that combination of genes could produce all the varying colors from jet black to snow white that we have in the world today.

---

[10] Ham, Snelling and Wieland, 141-143.
[11] Ham, Snelling and Wieland, 143.

7

Disproving Racist Lies

We can see that Adam and Eve must have been mid-brown in skin color to have the genetic coding for white and black descendants. But remember that God is a Spirit and He does not have a physical body. So He could not have given to Adam His own genetic color code, because He does not have a color. Therefore, when He created Adam and Eve, He had to make them mid-brown and place within them the genetic coding to produce every color of person there has ever been in the history of the world.

To examine this further, since Eve came out of Adam, let's begin by looking at Adam's genetic coding. Adam, as we know, did not begin as a baby and grow into manhood; God created Adam fully developed. If Adam was fully developed, was his genetic structure fully developed? Genesis 1:1, 9-12 may shed some light on this:

> **In the beginning God created the heavens and the earth....**
>
> **Then God said, "Let the waters under the heavens be gathered together into one place, and let the dry land appear"; and it was so.**

And God called the dry land Earth, and the gathering together of the waters He called Seas. And God saw that it was good.

Then God said, "Let the earth bring forth grass, the herb that yields seed, and the fruit tree that yields fruit according to its kind, whose seed is in itself, on the earth"; and it was so.

And the earth brought forth grass, the herb that yields seed according to its kind, and the tree that yields fruit, whose seed is in itself according to its kind. And God saw that it was good.

Verse 11 tells us God said:

... "Let the earth bring forth grass...."

Notice that God did not say, "Let there be grass," He said, ... **"Let the earth bring forth grass...."** Since the earth could not have brought forth anything that it did not already have, this tells us that when God created the heavens and the earth, He must have put into the earth the genetic coding for all plants, trees and vegetation, so that at a certain time, He could say, **"bring forth."**

If God did that for the ground, why wouldn't He follow the same principle with Adam?

I submit to you that when God created Adam, He placed in Adam the genetic coding for all the colors of all the people who were ultimately going to inhabit the planet. All Adam had to do was to procreate, or come together, with Eve (who had the same genetic coding as Adam, since the Bible tells us that God created her from Adam's rib), and they would begin the genetic cycle. Since Adam was created fully grown, everything that Adam had in him—his cells, brain, eyes, circulatory system, heart, lungs, every part of him—God must have put in him when He created him. So if there is such a thing as genetics—and we know there is—if there is any such thing as DNA —and we know there is—God had to put all the genetic coding in Adam when He created him. As a result, Adam and Eve had to be mid-brown; they could not have been white.

We have seen from *Strong's Concordance* that the word *Adam* means flushed in the face, ruddy or red. Many white theologians say this refers to a white person blushing, so that his white skin turns a rosy color. But when a person blushes, his skin does not stay that way; *ruddy* refers to a color, a reddish copper-brown. For almost 400 years in America, the white church has been interpreting this to mean that the man Adam was white and rosy-faced when he flushed or blushed—but genetics does not support this interpretation.

Let me show you how far some people will go to prove that Adam and Eve were white. "Scriptures for America Worldwide" identifies itself on the Internet as follows:

> Scriptures for America Worldwide is an international outreach ministry of the LaPorte Church of Christ and is directed by Pastor Peter J. Peters. This ministry is dedicated to proclaiming the true Gospel of Christ Jesus throughout the earth, and to revealing to Americans and the Western Nations their true Biblical Identity.[1]

(Note the term, *Western Nations*; apparently, to those behind Scriptures for America Worldwide, Eastern nations do not count.)

In a section entitled, "Frequently Asked Questions and Answers," I found the question:

> What about Adam and Eve? Were they of the white 'race' or are they the mother and father of all the "races"?[2]

---

1 See Scriptures for America Worldwide at: pastor@christianidentity.org.

2 Scriptures for America Worldwide, "Continued from FAQ–Israel Identity, pt 2," no. 11, page 1 of 10, last updated 2/20/95.

The implications are clear: there are two separate races, the white race and the mongrels; and Adam and Eve are not the mother and father of all the races, they are only the mother and father of the white race.

In fact, Scriptures for America Worldwide goes on to state that "Adam was White."[3] It elaborates by saying, "Adam was fair and white which caused the hemoglobin (blood) to show in his skin making him look 'ruddy' or to give him a 'flush' look."[4] Later we are told on this site:

> That Adam and Eve were of the white race with this fair, ruddy or rosy complexion is verified in the Bible by the description of their descendants.[5]

Obviously the people who wrote this do not mean the colored descendants—the black, red, yellow or brown. They are talking only about white descendants. And they have more to say on the subject:

> Were they [Adam and Eve] of the white 'race' or are they the mother and father of all "the races"?
>
> Where does the idea come from that believes Adam and Eve were the only (first) two people on God's created earth? Both Creationists and Evolutionists agree with this false assumption. Both positions are wrong, but their adherents stubbornly cling to this concept as the only possible explanation when the truth lies elsewhere. The hypocrisy of the creationist's rejection of evolution should be self evident when they claim that all men have sprung from the single pair (Adam and Eve).[6]

---

3 Scriptures for America Worldwide, #1, page 1 of 10.
4 Scriptures for America Worldwide, #1, page 1 of 10.
5 Scriptures for America Worldwide, #1, pages 1-2 of 10.
6 Scriptures for America Worldwide, #2, page 2 of 10.

Take note of the fact that the evolutionists and some creationists do not say that all of us sprang from Adam and Eve, the Bible does. The group Scriptures for America Worldwide is claiming that the Bible does not. And if, as they suggest, Adam and Eve were not the first and only man and woman that God created, there should be some biblical evidence of it. But there isn't.

Genesis 1:26 states:

> **Then God said, "Let Us make man in Our image, according to Our likeness; let them** [that is, man] **have dominion over the fish of the sea, over the birds of the air, and over the cattle, over all the earth and over every creeping thing that creeps on the earth."**

Let's look at this again. The Bible says: **Then God said, "Let Us make man...."** Notice it does not say, "Let us make white man, black man, red man, yellow man and brown man." It does not even say, "Let us make Adam." It says, **"Let Us make man...."**

Genesis 1:27 tells us:

> **So God created man in His own image; in the image of God He created him** [him refers to man]**; male and female He created them** [because females are still man].

Why are male and female *him*? Because *him* is *man;* in other words, *mankind.* It says in Genesis 1:28-29:

> **Then God blessed them** [male and female; man]**, and God said to them, "Be fruitful and multiply; fill the earth and subdue it; have dominion over the fish of the sea, over the birds of the air, and over every living thing that moves on the earth."**
>
> **And God said, "See, I have given you** [*you* refers to mankind] **every herb that yields seed which is on the face of all the earth, and every tree whose fruit yields seed; to you it shall be for food."**

There is a point here I would like to clarify: Chapter One of Genesis tells us what God did; Chapter Two tells us how God did it. The Bible may look as if it is telling the same story twice, but it is not. Chapter One is like a skeleton, Chapter Two puts the meat on the bones.

Let's look again at Genesis 2:7:

> **And the LORD God formed man of the dust of the ground, and breathed into his nostrils the breath of life; and man became a living being**. [The traditional *King James* says *soul.*]

Genesis 2:8 says:

> **The LORD God planted a garden eastward in Eden, and there He put the man whom He had formed.**

The *man* in 2:8 is the same as *man* in 2:7, and the same as *man* in 1:26. Genesis 2:15-18 also tells us about the same man:

> **Then the LORD God took the man and put him in the garden of Eden to tend and keep it.**
>
> **And the LORD God commanded the man, saying, "Of every tree of the garden you may freely eat;**
>
> **"but of the tree of the knowledge of good and evil you shall not eat, for in the day that you eat of it you shall surely die."**
>
> **And the LORD God said, "It is not good that man should be alone; I will make him a helper comparable to him."**

As we know from our initial discussion of the word, *Adam* also means mankind. If you are a male, you are *Adam;* if you are female, you are *Adam*. *Adam* is different from dog, cat, fish and bird; *Adam* is all mankind.

In Genesis 2:19-20, it says:

> **Out of the ground the LORD God formed every beast of the field and every bird of the air, and brought them to Adam** [or to the man] **to see what he would call them. And whatever Adam** [the man] **called each living creature, that was its name.**
>
> **So Adam gave names to all cattle, to the birds of the air, and to every beast of the field. But for Adam there was not found a helper comparable to him.**

To show that Adam in this Scripture is the same man as in Genesis 1:26, let's go to Genesis 2:18, which states:

> **And the LORD God said, "It is not good that man should be alone; I will make him a helper comparable to him."**

Genesis 2:21-22 states:

> **And the LORD God caused a deep sleep to fall on Adam, and he slept; and He took one of his** [that is, Adam's] **ribs, and closed up the flesh in its place.**
>
> **Then the rib which the LORD God had taken from man** [or Adam] **He made into a woman, and He brought her to the man.**

Let's look again at Genesis 2:22 and also part of 2:23:

> **Then the rib which the LORD God had taken from man He made into a woman, and He brought her to the man.**
>
> **And Adam said….**

This makes it crystal clear that "Adam" and "the man" are the same. And we know that the woman was named Eve. So through the Scriptures we have followed God through the very inception of the creation of man—and the only man He created was Adam, and from Adam He created Eve. So Adam and Eve must be the father and mother of all the races.

Some racists have gone so far as to say that black people were an extracurricular creation that did not come from Adam and Eve, but from somewhere else. When you read the Book of Genesis, you might be tempted to believe this lie if you do not know certain basic principles, because people obviously come from somewhere. But if we read the Bible carefully, we see that it tells us where all people come from.

In Genesis 4:1-2, it says:

> **Now Adam knew Eve his wife, and she conceived and bore Cain, and said, "I have acquired a man from the LORD."**
>
> **Then she bore again, this time his brother Abel. Now Abel was a keeper of sheep, but Cain was a tiller of the ground.**

Without going into detail about the story of Cain and Abel, I will summarize it by saying that Cain rose up out of jealousy and envy and killed his brother Abel. After this, Genesis 4:16-17 tells us:

> **Then Cain went out from the presence of the LORD and dwelt in the land of Nod on the east of Eden.**
>
> **And Cain knew his wife, and she conceived and bore Enoch....**

People have wondered where Cain got his wife, because at this point in the Scriptures, nothing is mentioned about Adam and Eve having any female children. Since the Bible does not mention female children here, some might think that perhaps there were other people besides Adam, Eve and Cain, and that Cain got his wife from among them. But the Bible does not mention other people, yet, as we will see, it does provide evidence that Cain did, indeed, marry a sister. In the very early days of the creation of man, brothers had to marry sisters, and *vice versa*. That is the only way the human race could propagate itself. After a certain period of time, it would no longer be necessary, and there would be a prohibition against it. But until the time that the population was large enough to sustain itself without brothers and sisters marrying, that practice took place.

Here's how we can prove that this explanation is correct. It says in Genesis 4:25:

> **And Adam knew his wife again, and she bore a son and named him Seth, "For God has appointed another seed for me instead of Abel, whom Cain killed."**

In Genesis 5:3-4, we learn:

> **And Adam lived one hundred and thirty years, and begot a son in his own likeness, after his image, and named him Seth.**
>
> **After he begot Seth, the days of Adam were eight hundred years; and he had sons and daughters.**

By name, the Bible only tells us about three children that Adam and Eve had: Cain, Abel and Seth. But Genesis 5:4 clearly tells us **... he had sons and daughters**. Verse 5 states:

> **So all the days that Adam lived were nine hundred and thirty years; and he died.**

Thus, in the 930 years that Adam lived, as Verse 5 points out, he had sons and daughters, not just the three sons named in the Bible.

We might wonder—and it would be a legitimate question—why the Bible doesn't tell us about the other children by name. The reason is that the Bible is not a history book in the way that we think about history: It is not a history of man on earth; it is the story of God dealing with mankind redemptively. Consequently, we will find that many historical events and figures are not mentioned in the Bible. For example, we know that Alexander the Great lived during biblical times and had enormous influence on the world, yet there is nothing about him in the Bible. Why? Because Alexander the Great had nothing to do with redemption. The only things listed specifically in the Bible are things that impact man's redemption.

Let's look again at Genesis 5:4:

> **After he begot Seth, the days of Adam were eight hundred years; and he had sons and daughters.**

As we saw before, no daughters are listed by name. In the Hebrew economy, when genealogies are given, they are always listed through the male, because the male carries the seed. If we go to the gospels of Matthew and Luke, and look at the genealogy of Jesus, we again find that only males are listed. We never hear about the females in genealogies, even though we know that women are part of procreation. If we go through the Book of Genesis from the beginning up until the Tower of Babel, over and over again we will find statements that a male lived so many hundreds of years and begot sons and daughters.

So when Cain went to the land of Nod, he married his sister, although we do not know her name; we know this because we know from the Bible that there was no one else to marry, and that he did, indeed, have sisters. I have shown from the Bible that Adam and Eve were the first and only two people that God created, and that everyone else descended from them. Genesis 3:20 absolutely confirms this when it says:

> **And Adam called his wife's name Eve, because she was the mother of all living.**

Notice this does not say "mother of all living Whites," but **... the mother of all living.** That means mother of all living Blacks,

Reds, Yellows, Browns and Whites. And that is why Adam and Eve were definitely mid-brown in complexion.

Racists will angrily respond to this, "No, Brother Price, you're wrong! You must remember that God cursed Ham, and his curse was blackness."

This is what has been taught for almost 400 years in this country by the Church: that the black color of our skin is the result of a curse on Ham. If this were so, then Adam and Eve could be white, because Ham's color would not have come from genetics, it would have come from the curse. *But there is no Scripture in the Bible that says God cursed Ham with blackness.* God never cursed Ham at all. Noah did the cursing—but it was not Ham he cursed, it was Ham's son Canaan. And Noah is not God. And God was not going to honor Noah, who probably was still hungover from drinking wine, by allowing his words against Canaan to affect Canaan and his descendants throughout all eternity (Genesis 9:21). As we have seen from the Scriptures, God does not curse anyone through all eternity.

I have another point to make to the racists: If God cursed Ham and the curse was blackness so that all of his children came out black, then what shade of black would they be? Black people come in every shade—but if God cursed Ham, it would mean that every cursed black person would have to be the same shade. If Ham were cursed jet black, then every one of his children and his children's children and their children's children down through the ages would have to be jet black. If Ham was cursed a lighter color black, then all of his descendants would have to be a lighter color black, and if the black color was a curse, then even if he married Snow White, their children would still be black because black is a curse. If Ham were cursed, the color could never change, because it would not be determined by genetics, it would be determined by the curse. The only way that a child could come out a different shade than a parent who carries the curse would be if the curse changed.

We know that none of this is the case. If a jet-black person marries a snow-white person from Scandinavia, their children may come out any color from very light to very dark. And if those children marry other children of their color, their children may be a lighter color than that. Besides all of this, the Bible tells us in Galatians 3:13:

> **Christ has redeemed us from the curse of the law, having become a curse for us....**

The ninth chapter of Genesis, which talks about Noah, is part of what is called The Law (besides Genesis, The Law also includes the other four books of the Pentateuch: Exodus, Leviticus, Numbers and Deuteronomy). If, as the Bible says, I am redeemed from the curse of the law through Christ, then, if blackness is a curse, the blackness of my skin ought to vanish and I ought to be another color. Christians, both white and black, have believed the lie of the curse for almost four centuries. It is a lie that came right out of the pit of hell, and that is where it needs to go—back to hell!

Black people are not cursed—and we are not an afterthought of God. We are in the equation; we are in the genes; we are in the DNA; we were in Adam and Eve. And as *The Answers Book* tells us, "most of the world's population today is still mid-brown in color."[7]

There are more mid-brown people than there are white people on this planet.

---

[7] Ham, Snelling and Wieland, 146.

8
The Underlying Reason for Racism

In our country, we throw around the word *race* as if different races of different colors existed from the beginning of time. We know from what we've seen in the previous chapter that Adam and Eve were mid-brown in color, and the different races developed from them. How did this happen? *The Answers Book* explains it as follows:

> After the Flood, for the few centuries until Babel, there was only one language and one culture group. Thus, there were no barriers to marriage within this group. This would tend to keep the skin color of the population away from the extremes. Very dark and very light skin would appear, of course, but people tending in either direction would be free to marry someone less dark or less light than themselves, ensuring that the average color stayed roughly the same. The same would be true of other characteristics, not just skin color. Under these sorts of circumstances, distinct racial lines will never emerge. This is true for animals as well as human populations, as every biologist knows. To obtain such separate lines, you would need to break a large breeding group into smaller groups and keep them separate, that is, not interbreeding any more.

> This is exactly what happened at Babel. Once separate languages were imposed [according to Genesis 11:9, **... the Lord confused the language of all the earth....**], there were instantaneous barriers. Not only would people tend not to marry someone they couldn't understand, but entire groups which spoke the same language would have difficulty relating to and trusting those which did not. They would tend to move away or be forced away from each other, into different environments. This, of course, is what God intended. It is unlikely that each small group would carry the same broad range of skin colors as the original, larger group. So one group might have more dark genes, on average, while another might have more light genes. The same thing would happen to other characteristics: nose shape, eye shape, etc. And since they would interbreed only within their own language group, this tendency would no longer be averaged out as before.[1]

So different races of different colors most probably came about after people separated into tribes after the introduction of different languages. The reason it is important to know where we came from is that where we are now is the result of where we started. We have to find accurate information so that we can better interpret why things are the way they are, and that is why it is necessary to expose the false racist teaching that Adam and Eve were white. As we have seen, it is simply not supported by biology.

Indeed, scientists are finding that the entire idea of race has no biological basis. An article in *The Los Angeles Times* informs us:

> Researchers adept at analyzing the genetic threads of human diversity said Sunday that the concept of race—the source of abiding cultural and political divisions in American society—simply has no basis in fundamental human biology.

---

[1] Ham, Snelling and Wieland, 146-147.

> Scientists should abandon it, they said.
>
> "Biologically, we are saying in essence that race is no longer a valid scientific distinction," said Solomon H. Katz, a University of Pennsylvania anthropologist.
>
> "Race is a social construct derived mainly from perceptions conditioned by events of recorded history, and it has no basic biological reality," said C. Loring Brace, a biological anthropologist at the University of Michigan.
>
> "The old biological definitions of race were based on what people looked like," said Joseph L. Graves Jr., an evolutionary biologist at Arizona State University West....
>
> "Social scientists are confronted with a dilemma in that they use racial categories in order to conduct their research studies, to compare and contrast life changes or social and economic progress; at the same time there is an understanding that race has no biological reality," said Michael Omi, an expert in ethnic studies at UC Berkeley.

This article ends with a comment made by Rhett Jones, director of Brown University's Center for the Study of Race:

> "Most White people—not all—really do believe that you can tell something about somebody by his or her skin color...."[2]

These are scientists of various ethnic backgrounds. And they are telling us, first, that race is not a valid concept biologically, and, second, that many Caucasians believe they can tell something about an individual from his or her skin color. That is

---

2 Robert Lee Hotz, "Scientists Say Race Has No Biological Basis," *Los Angeles Times*, Home ed., v. CXIV, no. 79, (Monday, February 20, 1995), A-1, A-10.

why so many Whites moved out of the inner cities. They believe that if you are a black person, in some way you have to be bad.

Many Whites who love and support my ministry will not come to the FaithDome. Viewers of my telecast have written to tell me that they don't go to church because they haven't found a church that ministers to them the way my program does. But they will not come to our church because it is in a black neighborhood and black people scare them. Their minds are so filled with media images of purported black violence that on some level they tend to categorize Blacks in a negative way, as if all black people are muggers and all black men rape white women.

The thing that irks me most is they are putting me in the same category as rapists, muggers and murderers. They are putting all of the black people who attend my church—who are born again and are filled with the Holy Spirit and who have their families together or are working on having their families together—in the same category as rapists, muggers and murderers, just because our skin is black. They are saying that all black people between where they live and the church are dangerous, just because they are black. That is the general perception.

Another commonly held stereotype, in keeping with images of our tribal ancestry, is that black people are highly sexual. Although this may be a projection of unadmitted white lust, some Whites subscribe to it and use it to fuel their paranoia about the mixing of the races.

Most black men have had the experience of waiting for an elevator and, when the door opens, seeing a white woman inside who emanates a sense of fear when she sees a black man about to walk into it. She fears she is going to get mugged or raped in the elevator, because that is a black man, and that is what they do. Every black man gets painted with the same brush.

As we noted earlier, we generally use the term *racism* to describe racial and color prejudice. But technically, prejudice and racism are two different things. Racism is about economics, not color.

The Underlying Reason for Racism

In *Uprooting Racism*, educator Paul Kivel, who happens to be white, makes some very illuminating observations about racism in the United States, as does black educator and economic development consultant Dr. Claud Anderson in his book, *Black Labor, White Wealth*. Taken together, these observations add another dimension to our study of racism and provide a solid foundation for the rest of our discussion.

As Kivel points out, "Our society has been built upon a foundation of racism for so long that it's become part of the landscape: always there, seldom acknowledged."[3] Kivel himself is intent not only on acknowledging racism but on exploring its many effects on all of us. He writes in his Preface:

> Before I wrote this book I accumulated a long list of reasons why it was an important project. Racism is pervasive, its effects devastating, the need to fight against it urgent. People of color are being blamed for our social problems and attacked on all fronts. Recent immigrants, African American women on welfare, youth of color, and affirmative action programs are just some of the current targets of white anger. It seems like gains we made in civil rights and social justice in the 1960s and 1970s are being rolled back in the 1980s and 1990s....[4]

And he goes on to say in the Introduction:

> As white people we do many things to survive the heat. We move to the suburbs, put bars on our windows, put locks on our hearts, and teach our children distrust for their own protection. We believe the enemy is "out there"—and we can be safe "in here." We never talk

---

[3] Paul Kivel, *Uprooting Racism: How White People Can Work for Racial Justice* (Gabriola Island, British Columbia: New Society Publishers, 1996), vi.

[4] Kivel, xi.

> about what it means to be "in here" with other White people and why we are so afraid of people with darker skin colors "out there."' Since we don't talk about our fears, we are precluded from doing anything effective to put out the fire.[5]

Kivel is an honest white man. I doubt seriously that he is alone among white people in the kind of thinking he describes. The only way that racism is ever going to be cleaned up in America is by admitting, as Kivel does, that it exists, and by taking action against it. I am a minister of the Gospel, so I am more interested in racism in the Church than I am in racism in society—but the Church, of course, is made up of society. How can we clean it up in one area without cleaning it up in the other?

Kivel's definition of racism gets right to the point:

> Racism is often described as a problem of prejudice. Prejudice is certainly one result of racism, and it fuels further acts of violence toward people of color. However the assumption of this book is that racism is the institutionalization of social injustice based on skin color, other physical characteristics, and cultural and religious difference. White racism is the uneven and unfair distribution of power, privilege, land and material goods favoring white people. Another way to state this is that white racism is a system in which people of color as a group are exploited and oppressed by white people as a group.[6]

White people must correct all the aspects of racism, including racial prejudice, and they cannot do it from the suburbs. If you want sugar and salt to affect the dish that you're cooking, you have to get the sugar and salt out of the sugar bowl and salt shaker and into the food. Staying out in the suburbs won't work; you have to

---

[5] Kivel, 1.

[6] Kivel, 2.

get in there where the pot is boiling, and that is what the Church has not done. The Church has abdicated its responsibility. As we know, predominantly white churches packed up and left the inner cities—but I hear Jesus saying, **"You are the salt of the earth."** What good is the salt in the salt shaker?

Since Whites were the ones who took the Church out to the suburbs, they are the ones who have to bring it back into the inner cities. Right now, there are no white churches in the ghettos—and we have to remember, the ghettos were not always ghettos; they did not become ghettos until the Whites left.

Kivel observes that "Racism and anti-Semitism are two primary, closely related tools that groups in power have used to maintain their advantage."[7] In analyzing the advantage racism provides for Whites, he comments:

> There are historically derived economic benefits too. All the land in this country was taken from Native Americans. Much of the infrastructure of this country was built by slave labor, incredibly low-paid labor, or by prison labor performed by men and women of color. Much of the housecleaning, childcare, cooking and maintenance of our society has been done by low-wage-earning women of color. Further property and material goods were appropriated by whites through the colonization of the West and Southwest throughout the 19th century, through the internment of Japanese Americans during World War II, through racial riots against people of color in the 18th, 19th and 20th centuries, and through an ongoing legacy of legal manipulation and exploitation. Today men and women and children of color still do the hardest, lowest paid, most dangerous work throughout the country. And we, white people, again depending on our relative economic circumstances, enjoy plentiful and

---

[7] Kivel, 3.

> inexpensive food, clothing and consumer goods because of that exploitation.[8]

Kivel is not afraid to talk about how the privileges that Whites enjoy were gained. In the following self-analysis, he describes the situation bluntly:

> It is not that white Americans have not worked hard and built much. We have. But we did not start out from scratch. We went to segregated schools and universities built with public money. We received school loans, V.A. loans, housing and auto loans when people of color were excluded or heavily discriminated against. We received federal jobs, military jobs and contracts when only whites were allowed. We were accepted into apprenticeships, training programs and unions when access for people of color was restricted or non-existent.[9]

Black people in America are an absolutely unique people. To have achieved what we have achieved with what we had to start with is truly miraculous! In 1865, when we were emancipated after the Civil War, each black male was supposed to get forty acres and a mule. Then John Wilkes Booth killed Abraham Lincoln, and the next president, Andrew Johnson, vetoed the idea, and we were emancipated with nothing.[10] We started out with nothing, and yet look what we have achieved!

We all know the game Monopoly. I decided to use this game as a test to prove my thesis that if you do not start out even with

---

[8] Kivel, 29.

[9] Kivel, 30.

[10] See David Warren Bowen, *Andrew Johnson and the Negro* (Knoxville: The University of Tennessee Press, 1989), 137. Bowen, referring to Andrew Johnson, states, "Near the end of his official tirade, he summed up his objections [to the bill promising land and a mule

every other player in the game, there is no way you can win.[11] Every player is supposed to get $1,500. I wanted to take the place of the slaves that were emancipated in 1865, who didn't get the forty acres or the mule, so I took nothing. I survived a few times around the board, but I could not buy any of the property I landed on and very soon I was out of the game.

We would all agree that it is unfair to have someone play Monopoly and not give them the required $1,500 to start with, but that is what this country did with black people when they emancipated us. And then many Whites have had the audacity to wonder why we have not done better. Whites started out with that $1,500 and Blacks started out with nothing, yet look what we have done! Blacks, be proud of yourselves. This is what Kivel is telling us when he talks about the economic advantages given to Whites by racism. And Kivel sums up the cause of all our racial problems in one succinct sentence: "Racism is caused by white people, by our attitudes, behaviors, practices and institutions."[12]

Racism is caused by people. This is why it can never be corrected in the Church or in society until those who have been

---

to freed male slaves] in a manner highlighting what he considered a clash between the interests of Whites ... and Blacks: 'In all our history, in all our experience as a people living under Federal and State law, no such system as that contemplated by the details of this bill, has ever before been proposed or adopted. They establish for the colored race safeguards which go infinitely beyond any that the General Government has ever provided for the white race. In fact, the distinction of race and color is by the bill made to operate in favor of the colored and against the white race.'" I will look at this in more detail in Chapter 13.

[11] This challenge was originally given during the "Vision Beyond the Dream Speech," Dr. Claud Anderson, Teaching Seminar, Crenshaw Christian Center, December 14, 1996.

[12] Kivel, 39.

perpetrating the crime admit to it, repent of it and make restitution. Again, Paul Kivel is a white man, not an angry black revolutionary. And his analysis of racism says it all: The real underlying reason for racism is not color, it is power. In that sense, the color issue is a smoke screen for the clandestine crippling of a whole nation of people for the economic benefit of another people.

Dr. Claud Anderson said something along similar lines when he spoke to a mostly black audience at Crenshaw Christian Center.

> "I want you to understand that we are in a highly competitive society and racism is the essence of competition. We are a noncompetitive people who must acquire competitive tools if we are to survive and prosper in this society. Contrary to what anybody tells you, racism is not about getting along; it's about getting ahead and getting over.
>
> "A few weeks ago, in the *Washington Post* newspaper, I read an editorial by a syndicated conservative black columnist on the issue of race relations. In reading the article, I finally understood why he nearly always comes down on the wrong side of racial issues. He does not know the difference between racism and personal prejudice and discrimination. He does not know the difference between racism and reacting to racism; nor is he knowledgeable of the true meaning of racism and who can qualify as a racist. Like most social pontificators, he perceives a black person reacting to white racism as a racist. A black person cannot be a racist!"[13]

Dr. Anderson is not saying black people cannot be prejudiced. He is not saying that Blacks cannot be bigots. But while anyone can

---

[13] "Powernomics," Dr. Claud Anderson, Teaching Seminar, Crenshaw Christian Center, May 29-30, 1997.

be prejudiced or bigoted, racism can only be practiced by people in the power position in society. As Dr. Anderson explained in an earlier seminar he taught at Crenshaw Christian Center:

> "Racism is a power relationship or struggle between groups of people who are competing for resources and political power. It is one group's use of wealth and power and resources to deprive, hurt, injure, and exploit another group to benefit itself. Racism in practice never existed on earth until the 16th century when white nations began to commercially enslave black people.
>
> "Black people cannot be racists because they do not have enough power and wealth to exploit, injure or marginalize white society or any other group. Moreover, there is not one recorded instance in our nation's history wherein black people have had sufficient wealth and power and attempted to use it to enslave, exploit or deny Whites the basic necessities of life. But, on the other hand, there are millions of instances wherein Whites have used their resources to kill, maim, exclude and marginalize Blacks.
>
> "Consequently, a black person can be a bigot and hate Whites, but he does not have the power to enslave, exclude or render white people noncompetitive. A black bigot can only react, march, protest and call white people a bunch of bad names. But this is not true with a white person. There is so much wealth and power concentrated within the white race.... [One group having the power position and using it against another group] is the true nature of racism and, like I said before, it began when the Whites commercialized slavery against Blacks back in the 16th century. Before that, there was no such thing as racism."[14]

---

[14] "Vision Beyond the Dream Speech," Dr. Claud Anderson.

There was slavery before that, but not racism; there is a big difference. That is why, as we have noted, slavery in America was called "the peculiar institution"—because no slavery anywhere in the world was or has ever been exactly like slavery in America, which was based on skin color. Most people, black and white, do not know this.

Dr. Anderson went on to say:

> "The root word of racism is race. Race, R-A-C-E, means to be in competition, in a contest or in a match for a prize or other group benefits.
>
> "Once a group has successfully won control over a sufficient amount of wealth and power, they can then institutionalize it into racism that automatically and systematically exploits, injures, or marginalizes another group by rendering them noncompetitive. Black enslavement not only displaced wealth out of Africa and into Europe, but it gave Whites a monopoly of wealth and power that makes it very easy for them to keep black people enslaved or noncompetitive.
>
> "Slavery is not new; racism is. Prior to the enslavement of black people, slaves were individuals who were the victims of religious persecution, prisoners of war, or personal indebtedness. Prior to the black enslavement practices, African Blacks were clearly not at war with European Whites, nor were they attempting to impose their religious beliefs on Whites. African Blacks were not monetarily indebted to them, either. Enslaving an entire continent of people forever based simply upon their skin color was unheard of."[15]

The system is stacked against Blacks, and if we do not pull together, we are going to be in the dugout, not on the playing field.

---

15 "Vision Beyond the Dream Speech," Dr. Claud Anderson.

Keeping people off the playing field is how you subjugate a people and keep them divided.

When Dr. Anderson commented: "Black people must learn to compete with Whites, Asians, Arabs and Hispanics; if we fail to compete, we will surely perish from the face of the earth just like any noncompetitive plant or animal," he was not talking about being against anyone; he was talking about banding together. It is the same thing I discussed in Part One of this book when I talked about black people having to learn to root for our own team. It is amazing to me that every other culture group can come together and everyone thinks it is fine, but when black people try to get together, the perception is that there is something wrong. That is part of the mind-set society has fostered to keep us so fragmented that we do not have any strength. It is part of the thinking that maintains racism.

9
Acknowledging the Past

When Kivel quantifies the destructive toll taken on Blacks during the early days of this nation through the end of the Civil War, the numbers are staggering:

> From 1619 until slavery ended officially in 1865, 10-15 million Africans were brought here, and another 30-35 million died in transport—a journey called the Middle Passage.[1] In all, 40-50 million Africans were abducted or killed by our white American and European fore-parents.[2]

We get upset, righteously indignant—and correctly so—when we think about Adolf Hitler and the annihilation of six million Jews during World War II. But who gets righteously indignant and upset about the fifty million black Africans who were abducted or killed by the forefathers of this nation?

If you ever go to Israel on a tour, the first stop will be the Holocaust Museum. Most people feel sick when they walk through the museum and see photographs of what one group of people did to another group of people, for no other reason than because of who they were. But where is the Holocaust Museum portraying

---

1 For these figures, Kivel cites Howard Zinn, *A People's History of the United States* (New York: Harper Colophon, 1980), 29.

2 Kivel, 121.

the abduction, rape, murder and enslaving of fifty million black Africans? The attitude of many is, "Forget them." People get upset when I discuss this, but they don't get upset with Jews for having a Holocaust Museum. And I agree with the Jews; thank God that museum is there. Hopefully enough people will go there and see that horror and never be tempted to do anything like that again or to let anything like that happen again to any group of people. But why is there no museum to commemorate the annihilation of black slaves and to teach the lesson that that should never be done again?

Kivel offers an interesting view of one of our most cherished heroes, Abraham Lincoln. Many Blacks and Whites have assumed that Abraham Lincoln freed the slaves because of a heartfelt desire to do what was right in the sight of God, rectifying man's inhumanity to man. But as Kivel shows us, we have been wrong:

> The Civil War was a complicated political, economic and social event, and while slavery was a key issue, the abolition of slavery was not a strong concern of the American public. As Lincoln wrote in a letter to Horace Greeley [a journalist and political leader of the day]:[3]
>
> "Dear Sir: I have not meant to leave any one in doubt.... My paramount object in this struggle is to save the Union, and is not either to save or destroy Slavery. If I could save the Union without freeing any slave, I would do it; and if I could save it by freeing all the slaves, I would do it; and if I could do it by freeing some and leaving others alone, I would also do that. What I do about Slavery and the colored race, I do because it helps to save this Union."[4]

This pattern of white society dealing with the rights of Blacks only when it is forced to has been passed on in America from genera-

---

3 Kivel, 121.

4 Kivel's source for this letter is Howard Zinn, *A People's History of the United States* (New York: Harper Colophon, 1980), 186.

tion to generation to generation. Many Whites do not talk about it openly, but they talk about it privately. And, as we have seen, many also have distorted ideas about black people. That is why racism has continued as long as it has, and the Church is the guiltiest group on the planet for fostering this kind of thinking. The Church has the Bible to tell them what is right, but not only has the Church failed to communicate clearly and loudly to the rest of the world that racism is a sin, it has not even applied this truth within itself. That is why in *All God's Children,* Steven L. McKenzie can say with truth:

> Despite the progress of the civil rights movement in the 1960s and the following decades, racism is still very much an issue in this country. Racial integration, which has crept into schools, businesses, and other institutions in America, tragically has made little headway in its churches. [Civil rights activist] Fannie Lou Hamer's observation about the Sunday morning church service being the most segregated hour in America is as true today as it was twenty years ago.[5]

Kivel makes an insightful statement that perhaps will make some people angry:

> [One of the problems] with "moving on" from slavery is that we rarely acknowledge the longlasting aftereffects of more than two hundred years of slavery. Although slavery was officially abolished by the Thirteenth Amendment in 1865, economic and cultural exploitation, everyday violence including lynching, rape, physical attack and other forms of mob violence, political disenfranchisement and almost total segregation in the South and the North continued into recent times. *We have had over three hundred and fifty years of economic*

---

[5] Steven L. McKenzie, *All God's Children: A Biblical Critique of Racism* (Louisville, Kentucky: Westminster John Knox Press, 1997), 122.

> *and cultural enrichment of the white community at the expense of African Americans* **[italics mine]**. The effects of that exploitation are in the present.[6]

There is a remark from Kivel that I think summarizes an important challenge in dealing with the issue of racism in America:

> We cannot build trust and an honest commitment to creating equality in this country if we are denying the injustices of the past. Our good faith efforts to change the system will not be taken seriously if we continue to deny or distort the record of white racism.[7]

This is a vital concept, and America has a lot to answer for in regards to racism. But as we know, America is not, and has not been, the only racist country on the planet. In South Africa, for example, the racist policy of apartheid was in practice for many years. It is interesting to read what South Africans themselves have said about the South African brand of racism.

In *The Churches and Racism: A Black South African Perspective*, which was written before apartheid was abolished,[8] Zolile Mbali confirms about apartheid what we have already seen about

---

[6] Kivel, 122.

[7] Kivel, 110.

[8] See Kofi Buenor Hadjor, *Dictionary of Third World Terms* (New York: Penguin Books, 1993). In his definition of apartheid, Professor Hadjor states, "The apartheid laws ... introduced a grotesque systematization of this pre-existing racial discrimination. The laws of apartheid included: the Population Registration Act, which registered all individuals by racial group; the Mixed Amenities Act, which codified racial segregation in public facilities; the Group Areas Act to segregate urban suburbs; the Immorality Act, which illegalized white-black marriages and sexual relations; and the establishment of the so-called Bantustans." He further reports that, "After the growing African resistance even the Nationalist Party government under President de Klerk announced in 1991 its

racism in our own country. "The economic reason for apartheid," he says, "can be seen as cheap labour.... The existence of cheap labour sustains the high standard of living of the whites."[9] Mbali, a black South African Anglican Priest, further states that, "The World Council of Churches' concern over racism goes back to the General Assembly held at Uppsala in 1968. Section IV of the Uppsala Report reads: (a) racism is linked with economic and political exploitation...."[10]

This is the same point that Kivel and Dr. Anderson have made: racism is about "economic and political exploitation." About apartheid, Mbali continues:

> We have sadly to recognize that in spite of the battle that has been fought against racism by the churches, mission agencies and councils of churches, with often heroic personal sacrifice, *racism is now a worse menace than ever*. We have also sadly to confess that churches have participated in racial discrimination. Many religious institutions *of the white northern world have benefited from racially exploitative economic systems*. Many church members are unaware of the facts of racism and of the involvement of their religious and secular institutions in its perpetuation. Lacking information about institutionalized racism and about the possibility of developing sophisticated strategies to secure racial justice, Christians often engage in irrelevant and timid efforts to improve race relations—too little and too late.[11]

Mbali supplies another piece of information that every American and every person who styles himself or herself a Christian should

---

intentions to abolish all the laws which had supported apartheid and the party declared the whole policy to have been a political mistake."

[9] Zolile Mbali, *The Churches and Racism: A Black South African Perspective* (London: SCM Press, Ltd., 1987), 11.

[10] Mbali, 15.

[11] Mbali, 18.

think about very seriously. Indeed, I think the future of our nation and the Church rests upon our comprehending the importance of Mbali's statement that, "Since its inception, the WCC (World Council of Churches) has consistently denounced the sin of racism."[12]

According to Mbali, the World Council of Churches is saying that racism is a sin. And if it is a sin, it should be repented of, and repentance means to stop doing it! That is one reason our nation is going through the hell it is going through; this nation has never repented. That is the bottom line: Racism called by any other name is still a sin! And sin must be dealt with! This is the statement that every church in every corner of the world should be making.

The question must be asked, how did America get into the position of being racist toward black people? We know that slavery was an economic proposition, but what were the conditions that allowed White Anglo Saxon Protestants—so-called Christian men and women—to condone racism and racial prejudice? What entered the minds of intelligent, rational people that caused them to mistreat a whole race of people who had never done anything negative to them? What allowed them to treat a whole race of people in a way in which they themselves would never want to be treated? The answer, of course, is the big lie that black people are inferior.

There is ample historical documentation to support what I have said in regard to the lie about the inferiority of Blacks. It is important to look at this documentation because if we do not know what causes our erroneous thinking about other people, we can never make any corrective adjustments. Before we discuss this documentation, however, I would like to address in more detail the reservations some African Americans have expressed about why I am dwelling not just on the racism and racial prejudice of today, but on slavery and other painful things of the past. It is a question I have been asked many times when I did the teachings on which this book is based, and that is why I want to answer it fully.

---

[12] Mbali, 17.

To my mind, *The Journey of the Songhai People* by Calvin R. Robinson, Redman Battle and Dr. Edward W. Robinson Jr., addresses this issue in a way that leaves little room for debate:

> Knowledge of race history is to the race exactly as an individual's memory is to that individual.
>
> The masses of African-Americans suffer from partial *cultural* amnesia because of a certain deliberate program which wiped the slates of our memories clean of true African events prior to the cotton fields of America.
>
> But the monsters who perpetrated this cultural genocide were not satisfied. After wiping the memory slates clean, they wrote upon those slates a series of vicious lies. They wrote on the slates, on the minds of all, Black and White alike, that the African is really an ape which can speak. They wrote on the slates, of the minds of all, that the African evolved in the heartland of the jungles of Africa where not even the faintest glimmer of the light of science and learning could penetrate. They wrote on those slates that this African sub-human has neither the genetic ability to learn nor the ability to behave properly. They programmed all of this upon the minds of all, Black and White alike.[13]

The history of our country certainly bears this out. The authors ask an important question and answer it superbly:

> "Why study modern history or any history at all?"...
>
> Two of the greatest benefits that can be derived from the knowledge of history is not only the receiving of a better understanding of the present, but more importantly, that

---

[13] Calvin R. Robinson, Redman Battle and Edward W. Robinson Jr., through the Pan African Federation Organization, *The Journey of the Songhai People* (Philadelphia: Farmer Press, 1987), 21.

> knowledge of history will provide the information with which to shape the future.
>
> Place yourself in the position of a successful businessman who, as a result of an accident, has a sudden loss of your memory. You would not know where your office is, nor how to get there. You would not know what successes you had achieved, what you are supposed to do today, nor how to plan for future successes. For all of your knowledge and experience would be entirely lost. You would have to start all over again. You would not know the reasons for your present situation. You could not call on experience and knowledge to plan for a successful future. If your business rivals stole your records, they could tell you all kinds of falsehoods. They could reduce you to an impoverished, blubbering idiot. That condition is called amnesia. Amnesia is not just limited to individuals. A whole race can have amnesia. It is a truism that "History is to the human race, what memory is to the individual."[14]

According to Cicero, the first century Roman writer, statesman, and orator:

> "There is very little that is more important for any people to know than their history, culture, traditions and language; for without such knowledge, one stands naked and defenseless before the world."[15]

We black people do not know our history, culture, traditions or language. All of our names are names taken from the slave masters. We do not know what our ancestors called us. The slave masters wiped the slates clean and that is why we have been defenseless. We do not know self because we do not know where we came from.

---

[14] Robinson, Battle and Robinson, 23-24.

[15] See Robinson, Battle and Robinson, 26.

And as the prominent American philosopher and educator George Santayana once said: "Those who cannot remember the past are condemned to repeat it."[16]

---

[16] George Santayana, *The Life of Reason*, 1905. Elizabeth Knowles, ed., *The Oxford Dictionary of Phrase, Saying, and Quotation* (New York: Oxford University Press, 1997).

10

Deprogramming the Brainwashing of Slavery

Let's look at some documentation on how the lie of black inferiority got started.

In *Infected Christianity,* Alan Davies discusses the work of the influential 18th Century Scottish philosopher David Hume. Hume, Davies informs us, writes:

> I am apt to suspect the negroes and in general all the other species of men (for there are four or five different kinds) to be naturally inferior to the whites. There never was a civilized nation of any other complexion than white, nor even any individual eminent either in action or speculation. No ingenious manufacturers amongst them, no arts, no sciences.[1]

Hume denies that there was ever a "civilized nation" of "negroes." He says Blacks are "naturally inferior" to Whites and implies that Blacks have the sophistication of apes. Yet many centuries before

---

1 Alan Davies, *Infected Christianity: A Study of Modern Racism* (Kingston and Montreal: McGill-Queen's University Press, 1988), 13.

Hume, the pyramids were built by black Egyptians, and modern science still does not know how the black Egyptians did it. In spite of the facts, to Hume, Blacks were just primitive people who had "no arts, no sciences."[2] These are the kinds of attitudes about black people that have been promulgated through time.

The perspective of many people today is much the same. If the attitude had been held only by Hume and by a few others in the 18th century, it would have died when they died. But those who have had this prejudiced and ignorant attitude about another branch of humanity have shared it with those around them. Often, people like Hume have shared their prejudiced views in writing, which, unfortunately, lends them an air of legitimacy. It has been passed on from generation to generation, through schools, through the Church, through books, through everything we have been exposed to.

As we will see, this attitude has been passed on to Blacks in America in a very systematic way, because it was part of the process of making our ancestors into good slaves.

In his book, *The Peculiar Institution,* Kenneth M. Stampp, Morrison Professor of History Emeritus at the University of California, Berkeley, and a specialist in 19th Century American history, makes this observation:

> Negroes ... had to be broken in to bondage ... carefully trained....

---

[2] What makes Hume's prejudiced and ignorant remarks so astounding is that educated Europeans like Hume knew about the pyramids long before Hume's birth. In the prior two centuries, several Europeans explored Egypt and wrote about their findings. In 1646, John Greaver, an astronomer from Oxford University in England, published "Pyramidographia," an important scientific attempt to measure the pyramids. See Mark Lehner, *The Complete Pyramids* (New York and London: Thames and Hudson, 1997), 44.

> How might this ideal be approached? The first step, advised those who wrote discourses on the management of slaves, was to establish and maintain strict discipline. An Arkansas master suggested the adoption of the "Army Regulations as to the discipline in Forts." "They must obey at all times, and under all circumstances, cheerfully ... that the slave should know that his master is to govern absolutely, and he is to obey implicitly...."
>
> The second step was to implant in the bondsmen themselves a consciousness of personal inferiority. They had "to know and keep their places," to "feel the difference between master and slave," to understand that bondage was their natural status. They had to feel that African ancestry tainted them....[3]

That is the reason so many Blacks are ashamed of their ancestry; we have been subtly, and not so subtly, programmed to think little of ourselves. Many Blacks don't want to know anything about Africa. Through the media, the power structure has primarily portrayed Africans as people running around in loincloths, bathing in the rivers, swinging from trees. Therefore, many Blacks have been ashamed of who we are as African Americans.

I know this to be a fact because until I got set free I used to be that way. I used to have a very strong inferiority complex. But I got rid of my low self-esteem more than forty years ago when I found out how to walk by faith (how to live according to what God's Word says rather than what the circumstances look like, how I feel, or what I think). That is what set me free. As I explained in Part One, I thought that once a person found out how to walk by

---

[3] Kenneth M. Stampp, *The Peculiar Institution: Slavery in the Ante-Bellum South* (New York: Alfred A. Knopf, Inc., 1956; reprint, New York: Vintage Books, 1964), 144-145 (page citations are to the reprint edition).

faith, he would rise above the pettiness of racism and racial, color and ethnic prejudice, but I found out that some people have never gotten free from that. And this is why I am doing what I believe God directed me to do: to reach people where they are by talking about these issues directly.

I know I am black, and I am proud of it; I am proud because God is proud of me because He made me black.

Dr. Stampp explains that slaves were conditioned to feel "that their color was a badge of degradation."[4] But this was not all. As he describes it, they were taught to degrade themselves in every possible way:

> In the country they were to show respect for even their master's nonslaveholding neighbors; in the towns they were to give way on the streets to the most wretched white man. The line between the races must never be crossed, for familiarity caused slaves to forget their lowly station and to become "impudent."[5]

It would have been impossible to teach these practices to Blacks without also teaching them to Whites; both would have had to be taught at the same time. And the teaching would have to be passed on from family to family, from generation to generation.

Dr. Stampp gives a capsulized account of training a person for slavery:

> Here, then, was the way to produce the perfect slave: accustom him to rigid discipline, demand from him unconditional submission, impress upon him his innate inferiority, develop in him a paralyzing fear of white men, train him to adopt the master's code of good behavior,

---

4 Stampp, 145.
5 Stampp, 145.

> and instill in him a sense of complete dependence. This, at least, was the goal.[6]

White society has done a masterful job on black people. As I mentioned earlier, many Blacks will not accept anything from another black man as having value until the white community has given its approval of it. That is because of the way we have been trained. We have no confidence in ourselves. We need to start developing that confidence now; we need to know that we are somebody—today!

The greatest building project of antiquity was the tower of Babel, engineered by a black man, Nimrod. In fact, it was such an enormously successful project that God Almighty Himself said (and I am paraphrasing), "I have to go down and check this out, because if I let Nimrod and his people alone, they're going to build a tower that reaches into heaven" (Genesis 11). It doesn't sound to me as if God was talking about ignorant people who didn't have any arts or sciences!

We Blacks need to know that about ourselves. We need to feel good about ourselves—not better than anyone else, just good about ourselves. Scientists shoot rockets to the moon; they shoot probes that are still out there traveling to their destination to the far reaches of our solar system. But they have not yet figured out how those ignorant Blacks built the pyramids of Egypt. To this day scientists don't know what system was used to get the huge, heavy stones to the top. And what about the design of the pyramids? They were mathematically constructed beyond the comprehension of the present-day mind; they were astronomically positioned thousands of years before there were any observatory telescopes.[7]

---

6 Stampp, 148.

7 See I.E.S. Edwards, *The Pyramids of Egypt* (New York: Penguin Book, 1947), 301. As Edwards reports, "The Great Pyramid was unique in making provision for the king to associate himself with both the circumpolar stars and the constellation of Orion and Sirius."

Consider the Great Pyramid at Giza. What a stupendous engineering project! Each side of the pyramid is approximately 755 feet at its base. That means it covers thirteen acres of ground. The pyramid is estimated to contain 2.3 to 2.5 million blocks of sandstone, averaging 2.5 tons each. Its original height was 481 feet, and despite centuries of weathering, it is nearly that tall now, making it the equivalent of a twenty-six-story building—and it was all built without cranes or other mechanized equipment.[8]

Every ethnic group needs to be made aware of the many marvelous contributions that black people have made to this country which are not part of most public education.[9]

We must stop believing the lie that Blacks are nothing. And once again, we must notice that the source of this belief is the big

---

[8] See Edwards, 143.

[9] See Mary Frances Berry and John W. Blassingame, *Long Memory: The Black Experience in America* (New York: Oxford University Press, 1982), 3, 32. According to Berry and Blassingame, today's American culture "continues to reflect in music, folktales, proverbs, dress, dance, medicine, language, food, architecture, art and religion the influences of West African culture brought here by African slaves." Suggested reading on this subject includes: Leon T. Ross and Kenneth A. Mimms, *African American Almanac: Day-by-Day Black History* (Jefferson, North Carolina: McFarland, 1997); Jack Salzmen, David Lionel Smith, and Cornel West, eds.: *Encyclopedia of African American Culture and History* (New York: MacMillian Library Reference, 1996); Walter L. Hawkin, *African American Biographies: Profiles of 558 Current Men and Women* (Jefferson, North Carolina: McFarland, 1992); Frederick Douglass, *My Bondage and My Freedom* (New York: Dover Publications, Inc., 1969); and Deirdre Mullane, ed., *Crossing The Danger Water: Three Hundred Years of African-American Writing* (New York: Anchor Books Doubleday, 1993). I will also discuss Blacks' accomplishments in further detail in a subsequent volume.

lie of inferiority that the white power structure taught to Blacks and Whites alike to maintain its control over slaves.[10]

Fox Butterfield, in his book *All God's Children*, points out an interesting fact:

> Before emancipation, virtually no records gave the surnames of slaves in South Carolina because, by law, slaves were deemed "chattels, personal in the hands of their owners." As a South Carolina court succinctly put it, "they are, generally speaking, not considered as persons but as things."[11]

That is how Blacks were perceived. That is why it was easy for slave owners to subjugate Blacks politically and economically—because a "thing" does not have consciousness or feelings. This was the *law* in South Carolina: Blacks were not persons, they were things. How could a thing feel good about itself?

I would like white people to ask themselves, how do you think Blacks feel? We have feelings just like white people. The Bible tells us: **And He has made from one blood every nation of men**

---

[10] In this context, it's interesting to note the accomplishments of Edward Alexander Bouchet, the first African American to graduate from Yale College. In the 1840s, Bouchet's father came to Yale as the personal slave of a white student. Thirty years later, in 1874, Bouchet graduated from the College. When he was awarded his doctorate in physics from Yale in 1876, Bouchet became the first African American to receive a Ph.D. Although he earned his Ph.D. in the first generation of his family to be freed from slavery, due to the prejudice Bouchet faced afterwards he was unable to find a job teaching at a university–despite superior credentials–and worked instead as a high school teacher and administrator. See Yale, December,1998, 14.

[11] Fox Butterfield, *All God's Children: The Bosket Family and the American Tradition of Violence* (New York: Alfred A. Knopf, 1995), 6.

to dwell on all the face of the earth… (Acts 17:26). Put yourself in a black person's shoes, and you will get a different perspective on the enormity of the wrong that has been perpetuated against black people in this country. It is bad enough to have been considered a "thing," but it is even worse that it was written into law that you are a thing. Where were the hearts of those who did this? Where was the Christ that they, as Christians, said they knew?

Black historian J. A. Rogers gives us another insight into how deeply embedded in American thinking the lie of black inferiority has been. In *Sex and Race,* Rogers quotes from a letter by Abraham Lincoln that is, perhaps, even more surprising in its content than the letter we have seen from Lincoln to Horace Greeley.

> Abraham Lincoln: "There is a natural disgust in the minds of nearly all white people at the idea of an indiscriminate amalgamation of the white and black races, and Judge Douglas evidently is basing his chief hope upon the chances of his being able to appropriate the benefit of the disgust for himself....
>
> "I am not, nor ever have been, in favor of bringing about in any way the social and political equality of the white and black races—that I am not, nor ever have been, in favor of making voters or jurors of Negroes, nor of qualifying them to intermarry with white people and I wish to say in addition to this that there is a physical difference between the white and black races which, I believe, will forever forbid the two races living together on terms of political and social equality. And inasmuch as they cannot so live while they remain together there must be the position of superior and I as much as any other man am in favor of having the superior position assigned to the white race."[12]

[12] J. A. Rogers, *Sex and Race: Why White and Black Mix in Spite of Opposition, 5th ed., Volume III* (St. Petersburg, Florida: Helga M. Rogers, 1944; reprint 1972), 41 (page citations are to the reprint edition). Rogers quotes from "Speeches & Letters by Abraham Lincoln," pp. 231,

There it is again: superior and inferior! Later, Rogers quotes a letter published in 1923, that was written by Albert Stowe Leecraft of Houston, Texas.

> "In animal life crossing of breeds produces what is called 'a Mule....'
>
> "A Mule-Nigger is the aftermath or fruitage of the clandestine visits of a low-down, depraved, degenerate white scallawag who by day lives in the midst of social refinement in the white communities of this Christian world and frequents the colored settlements under the cover of darkness of the night and plants his seed of iniquity secretly, with only the eyes of the recording angel watching his footsteps, and those human skunks well know the inevitable birth of their progenies brings disgrace to decent humanity.
>
> "A child brought into life through such a union of mixed bloods of 'strange flesh' is neither a white child or a Nigger; he is not white and he is not black, and the offspring of social error does not inherit the spiritual blessing of God or the fellowship of man.... He is a social outcast of society, a living monument in the walks of life, visualizing the abortion of the plans of God Almighty and picturing the perfidy of immoral humanity....
>
> "The laws of nature do not permit the cross-breeding of foreign seeds of life.... A coating of tar will not make an ink-spot white, and a million years of evolution will never bring forth a clean, pure, spotless-skin white child after the ancestral blood has been polluted with blood of Negroid taint....

---

369 (1920), Nicolay & Hay, 2 vols., and notes that "This was a very favorite quotation by southern politicians [at that time], and appears often in the Congressional Record."

> "The big, burly, flat-footed, thick-lipped, spread-nose, black-skin, kinky-haired 'Nigger' of this age are all of the blood of Cain, the man God made black."[13]

Leecraft's letter was from 1923, but consider how much racial hatred remains among some Whites, when in 1998 three of them accosted a black man named James Byrd Jr., tied him to a truck in Jasper, Texas, and dragged him to his death.[14]

In *Beyond the Rivers of Ethiopia*, Dr. Mensa Otabil makes several illuminating comments about racism and how it works.

> The spirit of racism thrives on misinformation and stereotyping. Instead of portraying people in the likeness of God, it seeks to devalue the worth of people who are different from us as not being as good as we are. Just because somebody does not talk the way you talk, dress the way you dress and look the way you look, does not in any way imply that they are inferior or superior to you. Different does not mean better.[15]

---

[13] Rogers, 45. Roger's cites his source of this information as *The Devil's Inkwell* (Houston: 1923), 33.

[14] See George E. Curry and Michelle McCalope, "Reduced to a Photo: A Family's Torment After the Tragic Dragging Death in Jasper, Texas," *Emerge: Black America's Newsmagazine*, May 1999, 42-47. On June 7, 1998, Byrd, a 50-year-old black man, was picked up by three white men who beat and then dragged him behind a truck for three miles to his death. The incident made the front page of major newspapers throughout the United States, including the *New York Times* and *Los Angeles Times*, and the brutality of the crime provoked a mass public outcry and commentary from President Bill Clinton. In reporting the event and its aftermath in May of 1999, *Emerge: Black America's Newsmagazine* stated, "There was a Ku Klux Klan rally in Jasper after Byrd's death, but such poison was not limited to Jasper." This article clearly illustrates that racism and racist acts continue to be committed.

[15] Dr. Mensa Otabil, *Beyond the Rivers of Ethiopia: A Biblical Revelation on God's Purpose for the Black Race* (Bakersfield, California: Pneuma Life Publishing, 1993), 12.

Dr. Otabil also points out:

Job said in Chapter 13, Verses 1 and 2 of his book:

> **"Lo, mine eye hath seen all this, mine ear hath heard and understood it, What ye know, the same do I know also: I am not inferior unto you."** (KJV)[16]

That is an awesome statement. Inferiority is developed when you do not see what someone else sees, hear what he hears, understand what he understands, or know what he knows. So then if any individual or group of people meant to dominate you, they would endeavor to manipulate what you see, hear and understand.

... When someone controls what you see, hear, understand and know, he can make you feel inferior about yourself and develop a sense of self-hatred and alienation.[17]

Self-hatred is one of the major reasons poor black youths have no sense of self-worth and see other Blacks as nothing. The majority of black crime is black-on-black crime, not black-on-white crime, because to Blacks, Whites have worth.[18] Whites are the ones who

---

[16] Otabil, 12.

[17] Otabil, 13.

[18] See *Uniform Crime Reports for the United States 1997* (Washington, D.C.: Federal Bureau of Investigation, U.S. Department of Justice, 1999), 19. The report states that of the 3,646 Blacks who were murdered in 1997, 3,388 of them were killed by other Blacks. Also see James F. Anderson, Laronistine Dyson and Tazinski Lee," Ridding the African-American Community of Black Gang Proliferation," *The Western Journal of Black Studies*, Summer 1996, 83-88. In this article, Anderson, an assistant professor of police studies at Eastern Kentucky University, Dyson, an associate director of administration at Kentucky State University, and Lee, an assistant professor of criminal justice at Mississippi Valley State University, address the rise of gang violence in African-American communities.

have indoctrinated us to feel inferior; because we do not see ourselves as valuable, we go out and blow each other away. We might as well be saying, "You're a dog anyway. You're nothing but a thick-lipped, wide-nosed nigger; I might as well shoot you." All of this has been programmed into us. Now it's time to erase that programming.

Dr. Otabil's observation about manipulating in order to dominate is expressed with horrifying detachment in this letter that was supposedly written by slave owner Willie Lynch in 1712. Although the letter cannot be authenticated,[19] the principles it outlines were practiced every day by thousands of slave masters on thousands upon thousands of slaves in one form or another.

> Gentlemen: I greet you here on the bank of the James River in the year of our lord, one thousand seven hundred and twelve. First, I shall thank you, the gentlemen of the colony of Virginia, for bringing me here. I am here to help you solve some of your problems with slaves. Your invitation reached me in my modest plantation in the West Indies where I have experimented with some of the newest and still the oldest method for control of slaves. Ancient Rome would envy us if my program is implemented. As our boat sailed south on the James River, named for our illustrious King James, whose Bible we cherish, I saw enough to know that your problem is not unique. While Rome used cords or wood as crosses for standing human bodies along the old highways in great numbers, you are here using the tree and the rope on occasion.
>
> I caught the whiff of a dead slave hanging from a tree a couple of miles back. You are losing valuable stock by hangings, you are having uprisings, slaves are running away, your crops are sometimes left in the fields

[19] Many years ago, I was given this letter by a friend. Today it is discussed on many Internet sites dealing with racism.

too long for maximum profit, you suffer occasional fires, your animals are killed, Gentlemen, you know what your problems are, I do not need to elaborate. I am not here to enumerate your problems; I am here to introduce you to a method of solving them.

In my bag, I have a fool proof method for controlling your slaves. I guarantee everyone of you that if installed it will control the slaves for at least 300 years. My method is simple, any member of your family or any overseer can use it.

I have outlined a number of differences among the slaves, and I take these differences and make them bigger. I use fear, distrust, and envy for control purposes. These methods have worked on my modest plantation in the West Indies, and it will work throughout the South. Take this simple little list of differences and think about them. On the top of my list is "age," but it is only there because it starts with an "A": The second is "color" or shade. There is intelligence, size, sex, size of plantation, attitude of owner, whether the slaves live in the valley, on a hill, east or west, north, south, have fine or coarse hair, or is tall or short. Now that you have a list of differences, I shall give you an outline of action–but before that, I shall assure you that distrust is stronger than trust, and envy is stronger than adulation, respect or admiration.

The black slave, after receiving this indoctrination, shall carry on and will become self-refueling and self-generating for hundreds of years, maybe thousands.

Don't forget you must pitch the old black versus the young black males, and the young black male against the old black male. You must use the dark skinned slaves versus the light skin slaves. You must use the female versus the male, and the male versus the female. You must always have your servants and overseers distrust

> all Blacks, but it is necessary that your slaves trust and depend on us.
>
> Gentlemen, these kits are your keys to control, use them. Never miss an opportunity. My plan is guaranteed, and the good thing about this plan is that if used intensely for one year the slave will remain perpetually distrustful.
>
> Thank you, Gentlemen.

As I noted, whether the Willie Lynch letter is authentic or not, everything it describes has been in operation here for almost 400 years. A lethal game has been played with black people and that game is still being played. The decline of the black male has been fostered by the rise of the black female. Those in power know, and have known, that the way to emasculate a man is to put him into a position where he cannot fend for himself, where he has a difficult time being a man and being the head of his household. So black females were hired over black males. This is still being done today, and men get to the point where they have no self-confidence, no self-worth.

The Willie Lynch "programming" has been worked on us so effectively that we cannot—or will not—work together. We have been brainwashed, and we have to change that. The idea has been insidiously planted in us to distrust each other, because if we ever get together, if we ever become one, we will become dangerous—dangerous in the sense that we will begin to take charge of our own destiny. Instead of relying on the white man, we will, for the first time in this country, rely upon our own abilities and our own resources. But as long as we remain dependent upon Whites, we will never come into our own as humans, or as true Christians who take pride in ourselves or in the God who created us.

There is another document that speaks to the condition in which slaves were kept, and without question, it can be validated. It is a speech on the abolition of slavery, given on January 16, 1832, by State Representative Henry Berry of Jefferson in the House of

Delegates of Virginia. Although Berry's attitude is condescending, he was an advocate of abolition, and had deep sympathy for black people because of how they were treated. Speaking of the treatment of slaves, Berry says:

> Pass as severe laws as you will, to keep these unfortunate creatures in ignorance, it is in vain, unless you can extinguish that spark of intellect which God has given them. Let any man who advocates slavery, examine the system of laws that we have adopted (from stern necessity it may be said,) towards these creatures, and he may shed a tear, upon that, and would to God, sir, the memory of it might thus be blotted out forever.

About America's treatment of slaves, Berry adds:

> ... We have, as far as possible, closed every avenue by which light might enter their minds; we have only to go one step further—to extinguish the capacity to see the light, and our work would be completed; they would then be reduced to the level of the beasts of the field, and we should be safe.

Keep in mind that Berry says America "closed every avenue"; in other words, our country did everything it could to keep the light from slaves. I am going to return to this.

> ... and I am not certain that we would not do it [extinguish the capacity to see the light], if we could find out the necessary process—and that under the plea of necessity. But, sir, this is impossible; and can man be in the midst of freemen; and not know what freedom is?[20]

I want to focus again on Berry's comment that "we have, as far as possible, closed every avenue...." Understand this: What

---

[20] From the Archives of the Legislature of the State of Virginia.

happened to black people in slavery was not an accident, it was a deliberate, premeditated plan to keep our ancestors ignorant so that they could be manipulated. No wonder so many of the descendants of people who were manipulated in this way have low self-esteem. And that is why I keep telling black people to recover themselves out of this low self-esteem. I've said it before and I'll say it again, we need to stop and realize how marvelous we actually are.

It really was against the law to teach a slave to read! Even after slavery was abolished in 1865, Whites did everything they could to keep Blacks from attending school.[21] And with all that has been done against us, look at what we have accomplished since that time. That ought to make us feel a little bit good about ourselves; not better than anyone else, just good about ourselves. Whites knew that if Blacks ever learned how to read, they would become dangerous. I am dangerous because I can read. We are all dangerous because we can read. And in this simple accomplishment, we have triumphed over the bigoted laws that racists wrote in our country's not-so-distant past.

All of this is documented, but most Americans never think about it. Some have never even learned about it. It ought to be taught in the ghetto schools; it ought to be part of the standard curriculum in *every* school from preschool through college. It needs to be taught

---

[21] For information about how the South in general opposed the education of Blacks after the Civil War, see Charles E. Wynes, ed., *The Negro in the South Since 1865: Selected Essays in American Negro History* (Alabama: University of Alabama Press, 1971), 138-139. Wynes reports that "when he appeared before the Joint Committee on Reconstruction, James D.B. DeBow said that Southerners generally laughed at the idea of Negro learning. They have become accustomed to the idea that the Negroes are pretty stupid.... Opposition to the education of the Negro was widespread. In 1866, the Florida superintendent of education said that the white people of that state cherished a deadly hatred to the education and elevation of the freedmen."

as part of the process of purging our country of the sin of racism and freeing Blacks and Whites alike from the programming that started with slavery.

This is what I want everyone reading this book to realize: Our whole nation is suffering because of the suffering of Blacks in America. I mean by this that to keep the black man down, the white man has got to keep his foot on him. Because of that, the white man is limited, too; he cannot go anywhere. We are all bound in a system of conflict and fear. Racist attitudes toward black people not only oppress black people, they keep black people from contributing what we could to our country if we were supported in fulfilling our potential in the same ways white people are. How many potential doctors, scientists, artists and teachers are not developing among today's youth in the black ghetto because of the low self-esteem and the lack of a sufficient educational system? How many young black people are not contributing what they could to the national economy because there are no jobs for them?[22] How many white people are stuck in their prejudice and do not grow as human beings as a result? How many people white and black are deprived of friendships that never take place because the color line is still so strong? Everyone suffers. The country cannot reach its potential because of this national sin.

---

[22] See Ronald E. Chennault, Joe L. Kincheloe, Shirley R. Steinberg, Nelson M. Rodrigues, eds., *White Reign: Deploying Whiteness in America* (New York: St. Martin's Press, 1998), 123-124. The editors report, "As realities of high unemployment, dire poverty, bad housing, poor-quality education, and dwindling social services are banished from public discourse, working class youths and youths of color are offered a future in which they will be earning less, working longer.... As American society reneges on its traditional promise of social and economic mobility for the marginalized and disadvantaged, it accelerates its war on the poor, immigrants, and Blacks while simultaneously scapegoating the young, especially urban Black youths."

11

Psychiatric, Medical and Constitutional Racism

To understand fully the obstacles black people have had to overcome in our society, we need to look at some additional viewpoints that over the last two hundred years have fed into racism and influenced public opinion.

In 1995, the Citizens Commission on Human Rights published a report entitled *Creating Racism: Psychiatry's Betrayal.* The report shows us how, since the last century and even earlier, racists have been creating shocking medical and psychiatric theories to support racist practices.

Under the heading, "How Psychiatry Lit the Racial Fires," we learn:

> The term eugenics was first coined by Francis Galton in 1869 in his book *Hereditary Genius*....
>
> In summary, the theory of eugenics posed that defective persons procreated more rapidly and bred more readily than normal, the result being that society was flooded with inferior and unproductive people. In 1870, psychologist Herbert Spencer took Galton's theme further

> by coining the term, "survival of the fittest," a phrase frequently and incorrectly attributed to Charles Darwin. Spencer believed many people were unfit and worthy only of a quick death, while selective breeding of the fittest could bring about a superior race.
>
> Director of the Kaiser Wilhelm Institute of Anthropology, Human Heredity, and Eugenics in Berlin, psychiatrist Eugen Fischer urged the annihilation of "Negro" children. Fischer theorized that blacks were devoid of value and useless for employment other than for "manual crafts."
>
> In 1939, Fischer lectured students, saying ... "I do not characterize every Jew as inferior, as Negroes are...."[1]

In other words, the doctor had a hierarchy of racial prejudice: some Jews were inferior and some were not; but all Negroes were inferior.

> Margaret Sanger, a eugenicist and the founder of Planned Parenthood of America, argued in 1939 for plans to stop the growth of black babies in the U.S. To cover up her plan to "exterminate the Negro population," she suggested that black ministers ... be hired to preach throughout the South that sterilization was a solution to poverty....
>
> The common thread to psychiatry's "scientific" justification for sterilization, brutal surgery and other human rights violations was that IQ regulated behavior and status.
>
> By the 1920s this was absolute dogma: IQ was congenital, inherited, and thus unchanging. In this way, the

---

1 "How Psychiatry Lit the Racial Fires," *Creating Racism: Psychiatry's Betrayal* (Los Angeles: Citizens Commission on Human Rights, 1995), 4-7.

> systematic social crippling of certain races could be carried out, if not by violent psychiatric treatments, then by denying them proper education, employment and other cultural advantages.
>
> Around the same period, a prominent "expert" in IQ testing, psychologist Lewis Terman, used his test to claim ... that children of the poor could never be educated, and that Mexicans, Indians and blacks "should never be allowed to reproduce...."
>
> The tendency of those who find it difficult to face such evil is to think that since those days we have entered more enlightened times. Unfortunately, this is just wishful thinking.
>
> In 1958, Audrey Shuey, author of the book *Psychology and Life*, wrote that IQ test scores "inevitably point to the presence of native [genetic] differences between Negroes and whites...." And this proposition has been spread even as recently as 1994 in Murray and Herrnstein's book, *The Bell Curve*, claiming that African Americans do worse than whites in intelligence tests, are "genetically disabled" and therefore cannot cope with the demands of contemporary American society.[2]

Superiority and inferiority—it is the same old story. In the section entitled "Psychiatric Oppression of African Americans," the report offers another interesting instance of scientific sleight of hand:

> When Africans were torn from their families and homes and sold into slavery in the United States, science stood ready to define any disobedience or insubordination by them as a "mental illness."
>
> As early as 1851, Samuel A. Cartwright, a prominent Louisiana physician, published an essay entitled "Report

[2] *Creating Racism: Psychiatry's Betrayal*, 7.

> on the diseases and physical peculiarities of the Negro race," in the "New Orleans and Surgical Journal." Cartwright claimed to have discovered two mental diseases peculiar to blacks, which he believed justified their enslavement. These were called *Drapetomania* and *Dysaesthesia Aethiopis*.
>
> The first term came from *drapetes*, a runaway slave, and mania, meaning mad or crazy. Cartwright claimed that this "disease" caused blacks to have an uncontrollable urge to run away from their "masters." The "treatment" for this "illness" was, "whipping the devil out of them."
>
> *Dysaesthesia Aethiopis* supposedly affected both mind and body....
>
> Much "scientific" and statistical rhetoric was used to justify slavery. One 1840 census "proved" that Blacks living under "unnatural conditions of freedom" in the North were more prone to insanity.[3]

Our present is the result of our past; the thinking of today has been influenced by the thinking of the past. The report goes on to say:

> Dr. Edward Jarvis, a specialist in mental disorders, used this [the finding that the North's "unnatural conditions of freedom" made Blacks living there more prone to insanity] to conclude that slavery shielded blacks from "some of the liabilities and dangers of active self-direction." The census was later found to be a racist facade in that many of the Northern towns credited with mentally deranged blacks had no black inhabitants at all!
>
> In 1797, the "father" of American psychiatry, Dr. Benjamin Rush–whose face today still adorns the seal of the American Psychiatric Association–declared that the color of Blacks was caused by a rare, congenital disease

---

3 *Creating Racism: Psychiatry's Betrayal*, 8.

> called "Negritude," which derived from leprosy. ...Rush said that the only evidence of a "cure" was when the skin color turned white.
>
> Using "disease" as the reason for segregation, Rush drew the conclusion that "Whites should not tyrannize over [blacks], for their disease should entitle them to a double portion of humanity. However, by the same token, whites should not intermarry with them, for this would tend to infect posterity with this 'disorder' ... attempts must be made to cure the disease."[4]

Until I read this, I had no idea that my skin color was ever considered a disease, and that, by implication, anyone who is not white would have been considered to have the disease to varying degrees.

Let's look at another vital piece of the history of racism: When the Constitution of the United States was drafted, it did not consider black people as whole persons. Article I, Section 2, Number 3, of our Constitution originally stated:

> Representatives and direct Taxes shall be apportioned among the several States which may be included within this Union, according to their respective Numbers, which shall be determined by adding to the whole Number of free Persons, including those bound to Service for a Term of Years, and excluding Indians not taxed, three-fifths of all other Persons.[5]

---

[4] *Creating Racism: Psychiatry's Betrayal*, 8.

[5] See Abraham L. Davis and Barbara Luck Graham, *The Supreme Court, Race, and Civil Rights* (Thousand Oaks: Sage Publications, Inc., 1995), 2. "Four provisions in the Constitution explicitly protected the institution of slavery. Article I, & 2, Clause 3—popularly known as the Three-Fifths Compromise—provided that each slave would be counted as three-fifths of a free person for the purposes of direct taxation and apportionment of seats in the House of Representatives."

Blacks were considered three-fifths of a person by the so-called Founding Fathers. Because of protests, this article was altered by the 14th Amendment,[6] so it does not read that way today, but we need to see how black people were defined at America's birth, because that conception fostered the present. Clearly, in the eyes of those who founded this country, black people had very little value as persons. And even though the Constitution has been amended, how many people still think that Blacks have only a fraction of the value of Whites? Not everyone thinks this, of course, but devastating damage has been done to the black psyche through the years of slavery and Jim Crowism,[7] which were supported by those who did see Blacks as having very little value.

It is not only a miracle that black people have achieved what we have achieved, it is a miracle that we have been able to maintain our sanity in the face of the kind of conspiracy perpetrated against us for these hundreds of years.

God must have a purpose for us.

---

[6] Davis and Graham,11, 60. "The Fourteenth Amendment, which was ratified on July 19, 1868, would become the chief legal weapon in black America's struggle for equality. Section 1 prohibits the states from (a) abridging the privileges or immunities of citizens of the United States; (b) depriving any person of life, liberty or property without due process of law; and (c) denying to any person within its jurisdiction equal protection of laws.... The Supreme Court's early restrictive interpretations of the Fourteenth Amendment, however, proved to be blacks' worst enemy from 1896 to the mid-1930s."

[7] Jim Crowism refers to the practice of discriminating against or segregating black people from white. For information about Jim Crow laws, see Abraham L. Davis and Barbara Luck Graham, *The Supreme Court, Race, and Civil Rights* (Thousand Oaks: Sage Publications, 1995); also see Catherine A. Barnes, *Journey From Jim Crow: The Desegregation of Southern Transit* (New York: Columbia University Press, 1983).

12
The Spiritual Basis of America's Problems

In *Free at Last?* Michael Goings comments:

> "Superiority complexes" constitute one of the major causes of racism in the Church and society. Although some would call this a psychological term, the fact is that this form of pride is perfectly described in the Book of Romans as "thinking of yourself more highly than you ought to."[1]

Let's look at Romans 12:3:

> **For I say, through the grace given to me, to everyone who is among you, not to think of himself more highly than he ought to think....**

This is a very interesting passage of Scripture, because it not only tells us what we ought *not* to do, by implication it also tells us

---

[1] Michael Goings, *Free at Last? The Reality of Racism in the Church* (Shippensburg, Pennsylvania: Treasure House, an imprint of Destiny Image Publishers, 1995), 16.

what we *ought* to do. This is telling us that all of us (**...everyone who is among you...**) ought to think highly of ourselves, but not think better of ourselves than we should, or feel we are better than someone else.

I want to repeat this biblical truth, because it is so difficult for many of us to fully grasp: We *ought* to feel good about ourselves. This Scripture provides the biblical foundation for why I say that all of us as human beings—black, red, yellow, brown and white—ought to feel good about ourselves. Of course, when we do, people may call us arrogant. But the Bible is telling us that we are supposed to think highly of ourselves. If we don't, who will?

Goings comments that "People with racist beliefs exaggerate their importance and ethnicity to overshadow the value of others who are different from them."[2] If someone exaggerates his importance and ethnicity, he is thinking of himself more highly than he ought to—and that is a sin, because it blatantly disobeys God's direct command.

Later, Goings makes another pointed statement:

> ... if racism in the Church is to ever be conquered, white believers (who constitute the vast majority of believers in the American population of the Church) need to realistically evaluate their attitudes about their black brethren and those of other minority groups. This superiority complex must be exposed and destroyed so that equality will abound and unity will be achieved.[3]

I know that for some white people, Goings' comment could be hurtful if it is taken personally. But, like myself, he is not dealing on a personal level. We are dealing with a system that needs to be changed. I know that not every white person supports the system, so if you don't, don't take this personally. But it is a known and accepted

---

[2] Goings, 16.
[3] Goings, 17.

fact that Whites dominate this country. They make the rules. They have the power. If there is anything wrong, they have to fix it, because they are the only ones who have the capacity to do so. They own everything. They control everything. So who else is going to fix it?

Goings strikes a nerve when he says:

> **Many Christians are guilty of the sin of racism because they don't realize that bigotry is a sin. Their minds have been blurred by cultural traditions passed down from generation to generation. This is especially true for many white Southerners who were taught from infancy that they were superior to African-Americans.[4]**

Notice that Goings says "many white Southerners." What are we going to do about this lie of superiority and inferiority that is believed by so many despite what the Bible has to say on the subject?

The thing that strikes me as so sad is that America calls itself a Christian nation and it doesn't even know what that means. America is Christian in name, but certainly not in action. And a tree is known by its fruit, not by its name.

People do not understand this, but it is a faulty spiritual base that is causing the problems we see in America. Many white people originally came to America to practice their religious beliefs without persecution. We had an opportunity in this nation to do it God's way, but when the Europeans arrived on this soil, they said, "Business as usual"; in fact, they said "We're going to improve on what we did in Europe; we're going to enslave a whole race of people."

First Samuel 16:7 tells us:

> **But the LORD said to Samuel, "Do not look at his appearance or at his physical stature, because I have**

---

[4] Goings, 80.

> **refused him. For the LORD does not see as man sees; for man looks at the outward appearance, but the LORD looks at the heart."**

Look at our country's history, and compare it to the Scripture: **"... for man looks at the outward appearance, but the LORD looks at the heart."** How could the white founders of this nation have called themselves Christians and yet turn people into slaves? How can Christians today who say they know Jesus Christ as Savior and Lord, and are filled with His Spirit, and who say that they walk (live) by God's Word, act from prejudice against other Christians because of their color? If you call God your Father, then you ought to act like Him. Instead of looking at my outward appearance, you should be looking at my heart.

Over three decades ago, Martin Luther King said this beautifully and movingly: "I have a dream ... that my four little children will one day live in a nation where they will not be judged by the color of their skin but by the content of their character."[5] That is what God does. Your outward appearance does not impress God, because He knows that outward appearance means nothing. Something can look beautiful on the outside and be nothing but rot on the inside. Case in point: Visit your local cemetery; few places are more outwardly beautiful in appearance, but under the green lawn there is nothing but decay and disintegrating bones.

Psalm 139:14 says:

> **I will praise You, for I am fearfully and wonderfully made; marvelous are Your works, and that my soul knows very well.**

---

[5] See Carolyn Calloway-Thomas and John Louis Lucaites, eds., *Martin Luther King Jr. and the Sermonic Power of Public Discourse* (Tuscaloosa: The University of Alabama Press, 1993), 114.

When the psalmist talks about being **fearfully and wonderfully made,** he is talking about man, and *all* of us are man—mankind. We are all **fearfully and wonderfully made** by God.

America is on dangerous ground. White America is on dangerous ground. It claims to believe the Bible; in fact, it has printed on all its money, "In God We Trust." If America trusts Him, why doesn't it believe Him and live by His Word? The way America acts, we should have printed on our money, "In Money We Trust."

Matthew 7:2 tells us:

> **"For with what judgment you judge, you will be judged; and with the measure you use, it will be measured back to you."**

It is coming back; your judgment is coming back, America. Read it and weep.

In Matthew 7:5, it says:

> **"Hypocrite! First remove the plank from your own eye, and then you will see clearly to remove the speck from your brother's eye."**

Acts 10:43 tells us:

> **"To Him all the prophets witness that, through His name, whoever believes in Him** [Christ] **will receive remission of sins."**

It says **"whoever believes in Him"**—it does not restrict it to white, black, red, yellow, brown, male, female, young or old; just "whoever." I am a whoever; what about you?

Let's look at 2 Corinthians, 5:16-17. These verses are powerful, and they show us exactly what is wrong with this nation that calls itself Christian.

> **Therefore, from now on, we regard no one according to the flesh…**

Before quoting the rest of the Scripture, I would like to note that as a teaching against racial prejudice—and as the right principle to have built our country on—we need no more than this. And yet the Scripture tells us even more:

> **Therefore, from now on, we regard no one according to the flesh. Even though we have known Christ according to the flesh, yet now we know Him thus no longer.**
>
> **Therefore, if anyone is in Christ, he is a new creation; old things have passed away; behold, all things have become new.**

What happened to the Church? The Church does regard according the flesh. The Church does not view everyone in Christ as a new creation, because many members of the Church carry their old prejudices with them. They have not yet let these old things pass away. I have said it before and I will say it again: the white people and the white churches left the inner city because of racial prejudice. The inner city used to be all white with small pockets here and there of Blacks and others. What happened? As more Blacks wanted to move into white neighborhoods, the Whites and their churches started looking after the flesh and moved out of the cities and into the developing suburbs. They were not looking at the character of the people moving into their neighborhoods, because if they had been, many of them would not have left. You may not have done this, and I may not have done this, but a lot of people did, and we need to look squarely at why they did in order to keep it from happening again.

What a wonderful witness we would make as Christians if the Church of the Lord Jesus Christ regarded no man after the flesh. What an impact it would make on the world. But the world has looked at the Church and the Church has been more divided, sectarian, racist and prejudiced than any other institution. The Ku Klux Klan looks like kindergartners compared to the Church. The Church has been perpetuating racism in America for almost 400 years.

Galatians 3:28 tells us:

There is neither Jew nor Greek, there is neither slave nor free, there is neither male nor female; for you are all one in Christ Jesus.

Something is wrong: The Church has not been following the Scriptures.

About 25 years ago, one of the largest publishers of religious materials in the world—if I revealed the name, it would be familiar to many people immediately—on the surface seemed to be Christian (I would think people who print religious materials ought to be religious), but their policies were not. I was informed by a reliable source that this publisher said they would "not publish a black man's book." Why? "Because no one is going to buy it."

Who wants to hear what a black person has to say? Forget what might be in the book; if it was by a black person, they would not print it. Forget about the quality of the teachings in it. Forget the anointing that God may have put on that black person's life to share the Word with others. Forget all that. They had a simple formula, and they stuck by it: "The author is black. We can't print it." Guess what? Today that has changed. That publisher found out that black people's dollars spend exactly like white people's dollars, and now that they have seen there is a black audience for Christian books, they will print Christian books by Blacks—not because of morality, but because of money. That is sick! And it is sinful!

First Timothy 5:21 is as strong an indictment of the way things have been done in America as we can find:

I charge you before God and the Lord Jesus Christ and the elect angels that you observe these things without prejudice, doing nothing with partiality.

On the basis of this Scripture alone, the white church in America should, metaphorically speaking, be sent to prison for life. In fact, it ought to have six life sentences running consecutively, because it has violated God's Word. It does things by partiality, and those in the Church who are guilty are going to have to answer to God.

Many Christians get righteously indignant about abortion, so much so that they are willing to protest in the streets, but they refuse to confront the racism right in their own churches. That is the epitome of hypocrisy. There should be a constant nationwide outcry against the sin of racism, just as we publicly protest against the sin of abortion.

When have white people protested in the streets against racism and racial prejudice in the Church? When did Baptists, Methodists, Presbyterians and Catholics go to the streets and protest slavery? Individual Christians protested and upheld the Word of God, but what about the Church as a total body?[6]

---

[6] For additional information about how the majority of churches supported slavery despite some church members' opposition to it, see Albert Barnes, *The Church and Slavery* (Philadelphia: Parry & McMillan, 1857), 9. Barnes, who was white, spoke out against slavery and the stance that religious leaders and denominations had been taking on the issue. He wrote, "I may make to show to my fellow-men the evils of the system, or promote universal emancipation, I am performing the appropriate duty of a Christian man, and of a minister of the Gospel." Throughout the book, Barnes expresses frustration and disgust with regard to racism, slavery and the myth of the curse of Ham. Also see Jon Butler and Harry S. Stout, *Religion in American History* (New York: Oxford University Press, 1998), 222. Butler and Stout report that George Armstrong, a Presbyterian minister in Norfolk, Virginia, wrote a book which offered a typical clergyman's defense of slavery. Armstrong's book, *The Christian Doctrine of Slavery*, written in the same year as Barnes' *The Church and Slavery*, contradicted that book and sanctioned slavery. See, too, Richard O. Curry, ed., *The Abolitionists: Reformers or Fanatics?* (New York: Holt, Rinehart & Winston, Inc., 1995), 67, which details the dissension among Baptist and Methodist churches during the "new abolitionism" of the 1830s, and explains how Northern members' support for anti-slavery increased while

First John 5:17 says, **All unrighteousness is sin....** Racism is a sin; racial, ethnic and color prejudice is a sin. So if you act in a prejudiced manner, or if you support racial discrimination, you are in sin.

I want to return to Galatians 2:11-14. I quoted this Scripture earlier, but let's look at it again as we near the end of this volume to re-examine what God has led me to do:

> **Now when Peter had come to Antioch, I withstood him to his face, because he was to be blamed;**
>
> **for before certain men came from James, he would eat with the Gentiles; but when they came, he withdrew and separated himself, fearing those who were of the circumcision.**
>
> **And the rest of the Jews also played the hypocrite with him, so that even Barnabas was carried away with their hypocrisy.**
>
> **But when I saw that they were not straightforward about the truth of the gospel, I said to Peter before them all, "If you, being a Jew, live in the manner of Gentiles and not as the Jews, why do you compel Gentiles to live as Jews?"**

Why did Paul call Peter on the carpet publicly? Because Peter's acts of hypocrisy and prejudice were done publicly, and therefore needed to be dealt with in public. I have mentioned that

---

Southern Baptists and Methodists remained entrenched in pro-slavery beliefs. Also see Mark A. Noll, ed., *Religion and American Politics: From the Colonial to the 1980s* (New York: Oxford University Press, 1990), 199-219, which states that the party of white rule in the South has perpetuated the racial polarity that continues to exist in American religion and politics.

some people, mostly black ministers, have criticized me because I challenged a white minister in a public forum because he spoke against interracial dating and marriage. The minister committed his offense in a public forum, so according to Galatians, that is where it ought to be challenged. I am exposing the minister's racism publicly, the Church's racism publicly, society's racism publicly, because that is where racism has been practiced; it has been talked about privately and planned privately, but executed in the public arena. And that is where it must be challenged if it is to be fixed.

In the next chapter, we will look at a concrete way to fix it.

13

What Our Country Can Do

We have seen that racism is a sin and must be repented of and stopped. In *Emerge: Black America's Newsmagazine*, Lori Robinson's article, "Righting a Wrong," is extremely thought-provoking in its suggestions for what America can do as part of the process of ending racism and healing the wounds it has caused.

> "Americans have difficulty dealing with the crime of slavery so much so that much of what is generated now in terms of the conservative atmosphere is undergirded by people who want to forget the past, who want to overthrow the responsibility for the past, who want to deny that legacy and its consequences," [says University of Maryland political scientist Ronald Walters]. "There is a direct line in terms of the consequences many Black people still suffer in America today because of slavery."
>
> That reparations is attracting more attention comes as no surprise to some African-American leaders.
>
> For African-Americans, the need is obvious, [Adjoa] Aiyetoro, [director of the National Conference of Black Lawyers] says. "The purpose of reparations is to repair

a people for significant harm that was done to them and particularly done to them by a government," she says. "One of the issues that we deal with every day is that the vestiges of our enslavement and post-enslavement treatment in this country has been such that it has beat us down as a people in so many ways.... Part of standing tall (as a people) is to say, 'You owe me for what you did and you need to pay.' "

Robert L. Woodson Sr., the conservative founder and president of the nonprofit Washington, D.C.-based National Center for Neighborhood Enterprise, couldn't disagree more.

"It's a waste of time and energy to be talking about reparations for something that happened so long ago," he says. "Why aren't we concentrating on going after sources of funds that represent our own money?"

But one reason many African-Americans haven't forgotten about the promise of 40 acres and a mule is that so many other people are collecting for past wrongs.[1]

On Jan. 12, 1865, three months before the Civil War officially ended, Union General William Sherman and Secretary of War Edwin M. Stanton met with 20 Black ministers in a Savannah, Ga., church. The ministers told them that freed Blacks needed land to sustain themselves. Sherman then produced a document, dated Jan. 16, 1865, which designated land for African-Americans. According to his Special Field Order No. 15: "The islands from Charleston south, the abandoned rice fields along the rivers for 30 miles back from the sea, and the country bordering the Saint John's River, Fla., are reserved and set apart for the settlement of the negroes now made free

---

1 Lori Robinson, "Righting a Wrong," *Emerge: Black America's Newsmagazine*, v. 8, no. 4 (February 1997), 44-45.

> by the acts of war and the proclamation of the President of the United States." Of the 4 million newly freed Blacks, about 40,000 would settle there, assuming they would become permanent owners.
>
> The original Freedmen's Bureau Act, passed by Congress on March 3, 1865, granted land "to every male citizen, whether refugee or freedman. As aforesaid, there shall be assigned not more than forty acres of such land, and the person to whom it was so assigned shall be protected in the use and enjoyment of the land for the term of three years at an annual rent not exceeding six per centum upon the value of such land.... At the end of said term, or at any time during said term, the occupants of any parcels so assigned may purchase the land...."
>
> The following month, five days after the Confederacy's surrender, President Abraham Lincoln was killed. His successor, Andrew Johnson, vetoed and amended Freedmen's Bureau Act in February 1866, which still called for 40 acres for "loyal refugees and freedmen," but changed the terms so the bureau's commissioner could determine the cost of rent and returning Whites could repossess their Black-occupied land.
>
> The Freedmen's Bureau Act that finally became law in July 1866 made no mention of 40 acres. To the contrary, it called for restoring land—about 850,000 acres of abandoned and confiscated real estate—to former White owners, many of whom had been accused of being traitors to the Union but were pardoned by President Johnson.[2]

This is history. But, again, most of us did not learn it in school. We may have learned that after the Civil War, promises were made

---

[2] Robinson, 48-49.

to freed slaves that were never fulfilled, but how many of us were taught the details of The Freedmen's Bureau Act of 1866? How many of us learned it contained legislation that would take away promised benefits from freed black men in order to return the benefits to white men, who had always been free, and who had built their fortunes on the lives—and deaths—of black slaves? If the details of the Freedmen's Bureau Act were taught at all, they were merely mentioned in passing; they were not emphasized as if they had real consequences for the current and future generations of black Americans, as indeed they do.

That is one of the reasons why I'm not surprised by Robinson's finding that, despite what our forebears suffered under racist laws, black people as a group today still have a hard time grappling with the idea of reparations.

> "I don't think [Black] people really understand reparations," says David H. Swinton, a Harvard-trained economist and president of historically Black Benedict College in Columbia, S.C. "They think it's somehow radical and un-American."[3]
>
> Nations are paying damages for injuries and wrongdoing with land and money. Making amends or giving satisfaction for a wrong or injury, as reparations is defined, is a standard practice in international law. The United Nations negotiates it.... Some nations even give it without prodding from foreign governments or institutions.
>
> In 1976, Australia gave its indigenous Aborigines more than 96,000 square miles of land after having appropriated it during European settlements in the 18th and 19th centuries. Four years later, Canada compensated Japanese-Canadians with $230 million for World War II internment and indigenous peoples

---

[3] Robinson, 45.

with 673,000 square kilometers of land after 13 years of negotiations over land treaty claims. In 1995, Austria promised Jewish Holocaust survivors $25 million, and about 10,000 people have received payments of $7,000 each so far.... Iraq will begin paying $300 million for every $1 billion in oil revenue to victims of the 1990 Kuwait invasion, according to terms arranged by the U.N. Security Council.

"There is some truth to those who argue that the modern debate over reparations was spawned during the formation of the state of Israel," says LCCR's Henderson.

Declared a state in 1948, six months after the United Nations voted for the partition of Palestine, Israel was forged on 8,020 square miles of land, some of which was occupied. In 1952, Germany began giving reparations to survivors of the Jewish Holocaust; by 1980, the amount totaled $58 billion in today's dollars.

Reparations, in fact, is very American. Since 1971, when indigenous Alaskans received nearly $1 billion and more than 44 million acres of land through the Alaska Native Claims Settlement Act, ethnic groups who have suffered mistreatment at the hands of the U.S. government have been demanding reparations and—except for African Americans—getting it. During the 1980s, five Native American nations were paid sums ranging from $12.3 million to $1.1 billion for stolen land and broken treaties. Most recently, the Clinton administration attempted unsuccessfully to win reparations from Cuba, through the intervention of the U.N. Security Council, for shooting down last February two civilian planes believed to have violated the nation's air space.

The Japanese-Americans' redress movement has become a model for African-American reparation activists. Raymond Jenkins, a Detroit activist known as "Reparations Ray," says, "Everybody thought it was a joke for years, thought I was a crackpot. They laughed themselves to

> death ... and when the Japanese got their $20,000 each, then they stopped laughing."[4]

This nation has the unmitigated gall to sit in chambers and discuss whether or not it should apologize to black people for raping them for almost 400 years. Think about that. And think about what the Bible tell us: **All unrighteousness is sin.**

Japanese people who lived in the United States were taken from their homes and put in internment camps from 1942 through 1944, because America was at war with Japan. Through negotiations, every Japanese American person to whom this happened received $20,000 and a formal apology.[5] And our government, our nation, is wondering whether or not it should apologize for enslaving blacks in America from 1619 to 1865!

The United States will not apologize to the best citizens it has ever had. Even with the racist policies of slavery and the racism that

---

[4] Robinson, 45.

[5] See Roger Daniels, *The Decision to Relocate the Japanese Americans* (Malabar, Florida: Robert E. Krieger Publishing Company, 1975), 136. "Appropriations of $1.5 billion should be made to the fund over a reasonable period to be determined by Congress. The fund should be used, first, to provide a one-time per capita compensatory payment of $20,000 to each of the approximately 60,000 surviving persons excluded from their places of residence pursuant to Executive Order 9066. The burden should be on the government to locate survivors, without requiring any application for payment and payment should be made to the oldest survivor first. After per capita payments, the remainder of the fund should be used for the public educational purposes as discussed in Recommendation #4. The fund should be administered by a Board, the majority of whose members are Americans of Japanese descent appointed by the President and confirmed by the Senate." Also see Dr. Mitchell G. Bard, *The Complete Idiot's Guide to World War II* (New York: Alpha Books, 1999), 356. Mitchell reports that, "From 1945-1954, the United States provided more than $35 billion in aid to Europe (mostly Britain, France, Italy, and West Germany) and nearly $9 billion to Asian and Pacific Nations."

has continued to be practiced against us, we have been as loyal as any other immigrant group that has ever come here. We have fought in every one of America's wars—and were treated like dogs after they were over. Sometimes we were even treated like dogs during the wars.[6] But we fought for our country anyway, were shot at and butchered and shed our blood for our country anyway, even though we were second-class citizens who could not even ride in the front of the bus or get a job when we came home—just because we were black. And our country has the audacity to debate whether or not it should apologize!

America has even paid money to the countries it has fought against in wars. Germany and Japan have built their economies on the aid they received from the United States after the last World War.[7] Maybe we Blacks ought to declare war on the United States; maybe that will get our country to give us reparations. Right is right. Our country says, "In God We Trust." What God? Where is right? Justice is not only blind in this nation, she is brain-dead!

---

[6] See Rhoda Lois Blumberg, *Civil Rights: The 1960s Freedom Struggle, Revised ed.* (Boston: Twayne Publishers, 1991), 23-24. According to Blumberg, professor of sociology at Rutgers University, "Black Americans have volunteered for every U.S. war despite the government's reluctance to utilize them in combat or provide equal treatment." Using World War I as an example, she states that, "They trained and fought in segregated units and often were allowed to perform only the menial tasks." She also reports that, "The end of the war saw the return of the armed forces from abroad, the resumption of the normal labor pool, and economic cutbacks. The nation no longer needed the labor of its 'last hired, first fired' black population."

[7] See John H. Backer, *The Decision to Divide Germany* (Durham, North Carolina: Duke University Press, 1978), 56. Referring to American loans and reparation payments to Germany after World War I, Backer states, "It should be viewed in the general framework of Germany's economy, which during the period 1924-1929 had a $1.5 billion foreign trade deficit, an additional outflow of about $2 billion in reparations, and nevertheless wound up with a balance-of-payments surplus

But as Robinson states, it's not only white people who have a problem with the idea of reparations, it's black people, too. Many black people I've spoken to have said to me, "We shouldn't talk about reparations; we should let it go." To me, this is foolishness. We are not asking for anything special; we are just asking the government, out of the milk of human kindness and Christian love and charity—out of fairness—to treat us as it did the Japanese Americans.

Japanese Americans were given reparations for having their property seized and being put in internment camps for two years. The racist treatment Blacks have experienced at the hands of our nation has been in force for almost four hundred years, and the American government has supported it without even the weak excuse that black people were of the same ethnicity as people with whom it was at war. After 246 years of slavery and 134 years of racism after slavery, how could our government still be discussing whether our country owes us compensation and a formal apology?

The white segment of the Church needs to read the following with care, because the vast majority of bankers, owners of manufacturing companies and corporate presidents are white, and because only whites—until the election of Barack Obama in 2008—had been presidents of this country. Whites are the ones with the power, and, as I've said, if anything is going to be fixed, they have to fix it, simply

---

of approximately $750 million." Also see Dr. Mitchell G. Bard, *The Complete Idiot's Guide to World War II* (New York: Alpha Books, 1999), 356. Bard reports that for the next nine years after World War II, the United States provided billions of dollars of aid to Italy, West Germany and Japan, the countries against whom we had fought in the war. According to Bard, "Soon most of these countries were exceeding their prewar levels of economic growth; and some, such as Japan, began several decades of exceptional prosperity. Germany's recovery was further assisted by agreements reached on resolving its World War I reparations debts. By agreeing to take token payments, the Allies showed they were willing to provide the loans Germany needed to rebuild its economy."

because they are the only ones who can. They have all the wealth. As Robinson's article in *Emerge: Black America's Newsmagazine* states, wealth itself is a core issue in reparations, because past racist policies are still affecting the economics of black families today.

> "The connection between the current status of somebody or the current wealth of somebody, and the future status, the way it turns out, is the way the economic system works," [Harvard-trained economist David Swinton] explains. "If you practice slavery, discrimination, racism, or any of those things for some period of time, it does have an impact on the future well-being of that group. It's not enough to just stop doing those things. Once you get behind in ownership of capital, the normal process of the economy will keep you behind forever." He defines capital as human capital, things that enable one to earn money, such as education and professional experience, and physical capital, assets such as financial holdings and ownerships.
>
> "The main consequence for future generations of current discrimination or past discrimination is that it reduces the capital of accumulation," Swinton says. "If it is desirable to equalize the status of the races in the future, then there must be some make-up, some compensation, some reparations, whatever you want to call it, for the capital that these groups were prevented from accumulating. Otherwise, the past will continue to perpetuate itself throughout the future."[8]

That is why reparations is so important: As we have seen, racism is all about economics. The color issue is a smoke screen for economics. There never would have been slavery if it had not paid dividends. But all these years later, black people are still paying a price for the dividends that white people reaped from slavery. "In God We Trust," "One nation under God," "With liberty and justice

---

[8] Robinson, 45.

for all": How can we as a country even pretend we are living these words when we have not trusted in God's Word that tells us racism is a sin? Or when instead of being "One nation under God," we are a nation that separates itself by the color of our skin? Or when there is liberty and justice only for those with white skin or enough money in their pocketbooks? I know that things are better now than they were a hundred years ago, and they should be, but they should have been better sooner, and they should be a lot better now.

In another article from *Emerge*: *Black America's Newsmagazine*, "On the Hill, Reparations Finds New Supporters," Kevin Merida reports:

> For the past eight years, one bill has proved too hot for floor debate, too hot for the hearings, simply too hot for Congress to touch—regardless of whether Republicans or Democrats are in charge.
>
> Known as the "Commission to Study Reparations Proposals for the African Americans Act," the legislation is introduced in the House every two years by Representative John Conyers (D-Mich.). It is his effort to force a national discussion about the lasting effects of slavery and whether descendants of American slaves should be compensated.[9]
>
> Conyers, who is beginning his 32nd year in the House and is the ranking Democrat on the Judiciary Committee, hasn't pushed the bill lately because he realizes there is virtually no chance of it moving in the Republican-controlled Congress. He couldn't even get the bill out of the Judiciary Committee when it was chaired by Democrat Jack Brooks of Texas. Republican Chairman Henry J. Hyde of Illinois is an even more formidable adversary.

---

[9] Kevin Merida, "On the Hill, Reparations Finds New Supporters," *Emerge: Black America's Newsmagazine*, v. 8, no. 4 (February 1997), 26.

> "The notion of collective guilt for what people did 160 years ago, that this generation should pay a debt for that generation, is an idea whose time has gone," Hyde says. "I never owned a slave. I never oppressed anybody. I don't know that I should have to pay for someone who did [own slaves] generations before I was born."[10]

If what Representative Hyde says makes sense, then none of us should pay for the national debt, or for the wars this nation has gotten us into. If you are an American citizen, you have to pay your dues; you have to pay your taxes.

I have the best illustration in the world: If someone dies and bequeaths a building or land to somebody else, the person who inherits it has to take it with all of the attendant liabilities; that is the law.

Another example, which I mentioned earlier, is that when we bought thirty-two acres in the heart of Los Angeles and built Crenshaw Christian Center, we had to pay $200,000 to the city in order to be connected to their sewer system. At the time we made the purchase, we were never told this financial assessment was already owed to the city for improvements that had been made. But nevertheless, since we had purchased the property, we had inherited this liability. The city's stance was simple: "It doesn't matter if the improvements were done before you got here or not, if you want to hook up to the sewer system, you will pay."

Any time you inherit anything, you inherit all the liabilities that go along with it. Of course, if you say that you will not accept your inheritance, then you are free. But if you accept it, you are obligated to pay the liabilities.

In the same way, if you inherit American citizenship or if you choose American citizenship, you inherit liability for everything

---

[10] Kevin Merida, 26.

this nation ever did at any time in the past, whether you participated in it directly yourself or not. I would think that being in Congress, Representative Hyde would know that.

14
Where We Stand Today

Right now we do not have legislation mandating reparations for black people in America. We do not even have a strong reparations movement. What we do have is a country in which racism is so much a part of the structure, that despite those souls working against it, the system keeps working in a racist manner.[1]

In an interview with *Modern Maturity* magazine, former Secretary of Education William J. Bennett makes an important observation about racism in this country:

> It's always worse for the underclass. But the middle class drives everything; everything trickles down. A common cold in suburbia is pneumonia in the inner city. If the middle class loosens its hold on marriage, the lowest

---

[1] See Carter A. Wilson, *Racism: From Slavery to Advanced Capitalism* (Thousand Oaks, California: Sage Publications, 1996), 6. Wilson explains how economic factors, which include the accumulation process, private property, and modes of production, have a major function in preserving racism as part of American society.

> economic class gives up on it altogether. The middle class fools around with cocaine and then goes to the Betty Ford Center. But Watts is destroyed.[2]

Bennett is not an angry black revolutionary; he is a white member of the establishment. Yet he is courageously telling the truth about the state of conditions for black people in our inner cities and how far we still have to go to eliminate racism from our society:

> The problem is, there's a blind, unconscious, beneath-the-surface racism in liberalism that tolerates this drug abuse and crime instead of blowing up the system that perpetuates the breakdown. People have to get really mad about this. If white kids were being slaughtered at the same rate as black kids, we would end the damn system. The country wouldn't stand for it. Black crime in America is intolerable for what it does to black people. And I'll be damned if the blame should fall mostly on the poor folks.[3]

Blaming the poor is part of the problem, part of our country's unwillingness to clean up its act and correct its racist ways. Like Representative Hyde who shrugged his shoulders and dismissed the whole idea of reparations, America shrugs at crime in the ghettos. "Since it's just those inferior Blacks, let them kill each other. In fact, if enough of them kill each other, we won't have to be bothered with them anymore." That's what America has said; only when violence hit the lily-white suburbs, with white teens killing white teens, was there a media and political frenzy about teenage violence. Violence is a sin, but so is racism—and being concerned about violence against white youth but not against

---

[2] Peter Ross Range, "Interview with William J. Bennett," *Modern Maturity*, v. 38, no. 2 (March-April 1995), 30.

[3] Range, 30.

black is a symptom of just how racist our country is. In America and in the Church of the Lord Jesus Christ, we better end racism before it ends us.

The following article also reports on this very present problem:

> The hot news from South Carolina last week came in a speech by Gov. David Beasley, who said the Confederate battle flag that flies over the state's capitol dome should be removed. He said a rash of black church burnings and other race-related violence have convinced him the flag has been so co-opted by hate groups that flying it brands the entire state racist.
>
> As always, the battle flag is a matter of some tenderness in South Carolina and other states where it is cherished by some as the symbol of a noble cause.
>
> Its champions regularly argue that those who associate the flag with slavery past and racism present are insensitive revisionists who don't understand.
>
> But those who crave understanding ought to be better at practicing it. As a matter of history, the flag was used to rally soldiers fighting for an economic system that was insupportable without slavery. The fact that thousands died beneath it gives no honor to the cause. Just more sorrow.
>
> Moreover, the flag is also a symbol of modern bigotry. South Carolina only decided to raise it officially in 1962, as a protest against desegregation. Other southern states took similar measures, and in each case, the in-your-face purpose was to support racial separation, to preserve the ways of Jim Crow. If no longer a symbol of slavery, the flag is nevertheless a lasting icon of hatred, not unlike the swastika.
>
> It's no wonder the red banner, divided by a blue cross containing 13 white stars, continues to stir such anger.

> However, it is a wonder– a greatly welcomed one–that Beasley has taken up the case against it. Beasley supported the flag's display during his 1994 election campaign. His new solution: Take it off the dome and fly it at a Confederate memorial instead.
>
> Maybe that'll work. Maybe by associating it more closely with the past, the flag will ignite fewer passions in the future. But removing the flag requires legislative approval, and although six former governors support Beasley's idea, the state's attorney general and other powerful leaders continue to resist.
>
> Their loyalty is misplaced. South Carolina's official state flag, featuring a crescent moon and a palmetto tree, was adopted in 1861 as the flag of the first secessionist State. Why fly a battle flag of war and hate when you already have one of greater principle? Is it pride? Obstinacy? Maybe just a lack of much needed understanding.[4]

The fact that Governor Beasley wanted to remove the Confederate flag from the capitol is a positive—if long overdue—sign of progress; the fact that the Confederate flag still has advocates who "regularly argue that those who associate the flag with slavery past and racism present are insensitive revisionists who don't understand" is a powerful illustration of racism's continuing hold today. It is also an example of the insidious and ignorant double-talk racists use to argue their indefensible positions.

In June of 1997, *Jet* magazine reported that "leaders of four major religious denominations in South Carolina recently issued a statement confessing to the sin of racism, and asking for forgiveness." The article goes on to say that this statement was issued after a two-day conference on racism in the church and that

---

4 "Good Move in Dixie: Governor Says Strike Flag," *USA Today*, Final ed., News Section (December 2, 1996), 13A.

among the topics discussed were the small number of Blacks in local and statewide church-leadership positions. *Jet* reports that, "The statement, signed by the bishops of the Lutheran, Anglican, Roman Catholic and United Methodist churches, asks Christ to 'help us in our struggles to overcome the sin of racism, the powerful prejudice which pits one race against the other to the damage of all.' "[5] The churches of these bishops have a total of more than 450,000 members.

Two years ago, the 15.6 million-member Southern Baptist Convention approved a similar statement apologizing for racism. These confessions of racism are laudable, and it is significant that finally some church leaders are accepting responsibility and are open to change. But for America to purge itself of racism, every bishop and every church—and every leader and every member of every church—must make the same confession and the same apology. And to do this, we need to put aside all double-talk and denial, and address the underlying mind-set that supports racism: the superior attitude of Whites toward Blacks whom they consider inferior. This is the root issue, and we must deal with it or it is going to haunt us to the grave.

Another recent article in *Jet* magazine, about a black actor being cast as Jesus Christ in "The Passion Play" in Union City, N.J., shows us that even amid a generally positive atmosphere, ugly voices of racial prejudice can still be heard shouting out their profanities.

> When he [the black actor] accepted the role of Jesus Christ in *The Passion Play*, he expected some stunned looks, maybe. After all, Desi Arnaz Giles has been acting long enough to know that being the first black man to portray the biblical figure in the Park Theater Performing Arts Center in Union City, N.J., would be breaking

---

5 "Religious Denominations in South Carolina Confess to Sin of Racism," *Jet*, v. 92, no. 3 (June 9, 1997), 27.

new ground. And not everyone would be exactly happy about the change in hue.

"As soon as you're cast in something like this, you know it may stir some people," Giles told *Jet*. "You know people are going to cancel. They're going to come to see Joe (Bukovec, the white actor with whom he alternates the role); you expect that. But death threats?"

Yes, death threats. After Giles was cast in the play's starring role, profane calls were made to the theater. It was reported that one would-be patron wanted to know, "when is the white actor playing. I don't want to see that Black thing." Another, spouting profanities, called the artistic director a "lowlife and a scumbag." And groups—including at least two church organizations—canceled their ticket orders.

The cast's response to the onslaught of negative public reaction? "Surprise," says the 34-year-old Giles.

Francine Trevens, the production's press agent, characterizes it as "shock. Because they've had a Hispanic play the role."

Although stupefied by the negative reaction to a Black man being cast as Jesus Christ, Giles says, his castmates have been in his corner throughout the ordeal.

"I think anything like this has to be stopped in the bud," says Trevens.

And although this is the first time in the 82-year history of the theater company's annual production of *The Passion Play* that the multicultural city has had to deal with the race issue, the overall reaction has been positive, says Giles.

"The positive re-enforcement, the positive support, outnumbers the negative at least 20-to-1," says Giles,

> adding, "I would say every actor prays for this kind of publicity."
>
> And the publicity has been good for ticket sales, which according to Trevens, are up approximately 20 percent. Additionally, once the negative publicity was reported, the theater began to receive numerous calls from patrons who called just to convey words of encouragement.
>
> But the thing that is really noteworthy, says Giles, is the fact that "last year I played Herod, (the king who, after Jesus was born, tried to have him killed by ordering all the children in Bethlehem slain), and nobody had a problem with that. And I played Lucifer (recently in another production), and nobody seemed to have a problem with that either. I guess they can accept a Black man in a negative role," says Giles. "But, I'm out to show them something different."[6]

Racial prejudice, which I have referred to under the general term *racism*, is, as I stated at the outset of this book, demonstrated most graphically in the issue of interracial marriage. Again, I am not personally advocating interracial marriage. My only question is, why should it make a difference if a White marries a Black or if a Black marries a White or if anyone from any ethnic group intermarries with anyone of any other ethnic group?

The reason it makes a difference to Whites regarding Blacks is that many Whites have been taught that Blacks are inferior and Whites are superior, and that superiority and inferiority are carried in the blood. Thus, if a superior white person marries an inferior black person, the black person's inferiority will be carried in the blood and transferred to any offspring, thereby tainting and diluting the superior blood of the white race. That is the bottom line.

---

6 "Black Jesus in Union City, NJ, `The Passion Play' Stirs Community Racism." *Jet*, v. 91, no. 18 (March 24, 1997), 12-13.

Where We Stand Today

Several years ago, I made a statement in the context of one of my televised messages concerning interracial marriage and I received a letter from one of the viewers that illustrates my point perfectly.

> Dear Sir:
>
> I have only one question to ask you. Let's suppose you have decided to go into business as your life's work, and to earn money to support your wife and children, and you've invested a large amount of money you've spent years saving up to go into this new business of your dreams. Let's suppose you've decided to raise a rare breed of beautiful dogs, which will sell for a high price when they multiply. Now you've got a beautiful female at the age of maturity and is ready to be bred—question! Will you let her loose in the alley so any old dog of any breed impregnate her? Or will you carefully find a dog of her high breed to impregnates her, so her dogs will be a purebred like she is, so her pups will sell for a high price? Thus, why would you tell your church to mix races and cause their children to be as mongrel dogs? Red birds cross only with red birds and oak trees cross only with oak trees, etc. So (us) ... why not see what God does with nature, which cannot choose otherwise, and just follow his wisdom and stay pure. I truly love each race and I want there to always be pure races—not just mixed people. Don't you?
>
> Yours in Christ,
> [Name withheld]

This is the racist posture. The white race is the purebred dog and all the rest of us are mongrels. Statements like this expose racism for the ignorance, bigotry and sin that it is. We read in the Bible that we are all made **"out of one blood."** All other opinions and concepts are racially prejudiced. Why would anyone want to go beyond God? How dare anyone go beyond God? If God made everyone out of one blood, black people cannot be anyone's mongrels!

I am going to present one last witness to the reality and presence of racism in America. It is from a commencement speech given at the University of California at San Diego, June 14,1997, by the President of the United States, William J. Clinton. The President stated:

> ... I believe the greatest challenge we face is also our greatest opportunity. Of all the questions of discrimination and prejudice that still exist in our society, the most perplexing one is the oldest, and in some ways today, the newest: The problem of race....
>
> Though minorities have more opportunities than ever today, we still see evidence of bigotry—from the desecration of houses of worship, whether they be churches, synagogues or mosques, to demeaning talk in corporate suites.
>
> There is still much work to be done by you, members of the class of 1997. But those who say we cannot transform the problem of prejudice into the promise of unity forget how far we have come, and I cannot believe they have ever seen a crowd like you.
>
> I grew up in the high drama of the Cold War, in the patriotic South. Black and white southerners alike wore our nation's uniform in defense of freedom against communism. They fought and died together, from Korea to Vietnam. But back home, I went to segregated schools, swam in segregated public pools, sat in all-white sections at the movies, and traveled through small towns in my state that still marked restrooms and water fountains "White" and "Colored."
>
> By the grace of God, I had a grandfather with just a grade school education, but the heart of a true American, who taught me that it [racism] was wrong. And by the grace of God, there were brave African Americans like Congressman John Lewis, who risked their lives time

and time again to make it right. And there were white Americans like Congressman Bob Filner, a freedom rider on the bus with John Lewis, in the long noble struggle for civil rights, who knew that it was a struggle to free white people, too.

... Let me say that I know that for many white Americans, this conversation may seem to exclude them or threaten them. That must not be so. I believe white Americans have just as much to gain as anyone else from being a part of this endeavor—much to gain from an America where we finally take responsibility for all our children so that they, at last, can be judged as Martin Luther King hoped, "Not by the color of their skin, but by the content of their character."[9]

---

[9] One America in the 21st Century: The President's Initiative on Race, June 14, 1997, The University of California at San Diego Commencement Address.

15
A Final Word

Before anyone pushes aside the president's address and the problem of racism and racial prejudice by claiming that African Americans have what they have and are what they are because of their own innate shortcomings, I would like you to consider some very important observations made by Dr. Claud Anderson in his book, *Black Labor, White Wealth:*

> It is common to hear Japanese, Chinese and Germans being cited as model hard workers. Before Blacks became obsolete as common laborers in the 1960s, they were the models for doing the hardest, dirtiest, most dangerous and backbreaking work. Ironically, conservatives and government are suggesting that emulating these recent immigrants and their hard work is the cure for Blacks' protracted poverty and high unemployment.
>
> Recommending more hard work for a race of ex-slaves is similar to curing an alcoholic by suggesting that the drunk do more drinking. Having never been compensated for centuries of past labor is the bigger part of the problem, not whether black people are willing to work hard.

A Final Word

If Blacks were unwilling to work, it would be understandable after 400 years of no pay to low pay.[1]

I hope you're reading with an attentive eye, because I am trying, as I believe God is leading me, to bring racism completely out in the open so we can deal with it. If we continue to sweep the critical issues under the carpet, we will never get rid of them. Black people need to realize that their ancestors—their great, great, great, great, great, great, great grandmothers and grandfathers—worked as slaves for 246 years without getting a paycheck, while white mothers and fathers and great-grandparents were accumulating wealth. Whites had a 246-year head start, and Whites wonder why Blacks have a hard time competing.

Think about it: From 1619, when the first slaves were introduced to the continental United States, to the end of the Civil War, there was no payday. And then from 1865 until the late 1960s, it was the lowest pay. And still the white power structure expects Blacks to compete. Whites still get on their high horses and get upset when we talk about how some of us can't make it. Let them turn the tables around and see where they would be if they had had the same experience in America since 1619 as we have had. "Which ethnic immigrants in America have worked harder than the black slaves?" Anderson asks. "Certainly the Japanese, Chinese, and Germans did not work harder in America than black slaves."[2]

Americans need to think about this before they criticize supposedly lazy Blacks. It is easy for people to find fault with others when they do not know, or refuse to acknowledge, the whole story. When people criticize us for being at the bottom of the economic totem pole, for being unwilling to pull our own weight, they seem to think that we

---

1 Claud Anderson, Ed.D., *Black Labor, White Wealth: The Search for Power and Economic Justice* (Bethesda, Maryland: PowerNomics Corporation, 1994), 97.

2 Anderson, 97.

Blacks are equal and therefore ought to achieve as everyone else does. That would only be true if we had all started out on the same footing, but, as we have seen in this book, that is not the case.

In a radio interview, Dr. Anderson was asked why Blacks in America have not achieved the way Asian, Hispanic and European immigrants have. His answer is enlightening:

> First, Blacks have never been treated the way European, Asian and Hispanic immigrants coming into this country have. Blacks have never received the preferential treatment of an ethnic group.
>
> Second, all of this nation's ethnic immigrants came to this country without the handicapping legacies and psychological baggage of having been enslaved and Jim Crowed.
>
> Third, all the ethnic immigrants came to this country voluntarily in the search for wealth and power-building opportunities. They were not dragged, bound and sold as unpaid, free labor to enrich everyone else.
>
> Fourth, they came in with their culture intact, and they were able to use their culture to create businesses and jobs. Their culture allowed them to build physical communities and maintain a broad sense of community. Their language, which is an index of culture, promoted unity by marking and closing their communities to other groups.
>
> Fifth, they came here with an intact religion that instilled a sense of spiritual values into their group, families and communities. Their religion helped them to acquire wealth and power.
>
> Sixth, even though they came to this country to acquire wealth, income and power, they were always free to leave or to use this nation's immigration laws to bring in other members of their families or ethnic group. By

> increasing their numbers, they could increase their wealth and power.[3]

I am sure that many Blacks as well as Whites have never thought about all of these factors. America wants black people to compete on an equal footing, but the obstacles we have been given are comparable to being entered in a 100-yard dash against an opponent who starts out at the ninety-yard mark while we are starting out at point zero. Then Whites cross the finish line first and stand there, asking, "How come you didn't do better in the race?"

I am dramatizing this because I want it to be perfectly clear.

The foul plant of racism has roots; we have to find those roots so that we can dig them up and destroy them, or else the plant will grow again. You can cut down a tree, or cut the grass or cut back the bushes, but if you don't pull out the roots, they will come back.

Whites want Blacks to compete on an equal footing when for generations and generations nothing has ever been equal between Whites and Blacks. How unfair!

Eighteenth-century British statesman and orator Edmund Burke is credited with saying, "The only thing necessary for the triumph of evil is for good men to do nothing."[4] Proverbs 29:2 tells us:

> **When the righteous are in authority, the people rejoice; but when a wicked man rules, the people groan.**

Our people are groaning, black and white alike. What are we going to do about it, America? Are we going to continue with business as usual—are we going to continue with it even though it is a sin—or are we going to rip up the poisonous plant of racism by its roots and destroy it once and for all?

---

[3] Interview with Carl Nelson, "Front Page" radio program, KJLH Radio, Los Angeles, California, 1997.

[4] John Bartlett, *Familiar Quotations 14th ed.* (Boston: Little Brown and Company, 1968), 454.

Appendix A

Below is the letter I received from a white minister (whom I'll call Pastor A) who learned of the tape with the apparently racist message on it and the subsequent breach between our church and the other ministry. Ironically, I received this letter the same week that some of the black board members of the Fellowship of Inner City Word of Faith Ministries (FICWFM) resigned because of my continuing to talk about the situation publicly. I had met Pastor A many years ago, and although I was well acquainted with his name, we really do not know each other personally. He wrote to me—and to the minister who made the tape—out of principle and out of a desire, like mine, to rid the Church of racism and the appearance of racism, and to heal the breach between the two ministries.

> Dear Dr. Price,
>
> A number of years ago, I had the opportunity of meeting you and sitting next to you at [a meeting of the minister who made the tape]. T.L. Osborne, a mutual friend, was one of the featured speakers that night and mentioned our church in Chicago, the largest multi-ethnic inner-city congregation in America, at that time. I've rejoiced greatly in the growth and success of your ministry through the years.
>
> It dismayed me that night as I watched your program to receive evidence of remarks made by [the unnamed minister] that were rumored a couple of years ago. It's tragic that racism still lingers in even the upper echelon of the faith movement. I've worked in Chicago for 23 years in the interests of racial harmony and reconciliation. I've rejoiced in the success of wonderful preachers in our city whom God has raised up to speak with authority to the

critical issues of our day. Reverend Bill Winston, whom you may be familiar with, was saved and filled with the Spirit under our ministry a number of years ago.

Today, I faxed [the minister who made the tape] a letter outlining what I felt is a proper course of action to help bring healing to the Body of Christ. I fear that unless swift and proper action is taken, the Body of Christ will suffer for years to come. I plead with you in the interests of the Kingdom of God that if [the minister] responds appropriately, we can all close ranks again and get on with the business of the Great Commission.

In the interest of the Kingdom,
[Pastor A]
Chicago, Illinois.

This is the letter he faxed to the minister who made the tape:

Dear [Minister]:

"Endeavoring to maintain the unity of the Spirit, in the bond of peace."

It's almost impossible for me to express how much the varied ministries of [you and your father] have meant to me through the years. I first met your father over 30 years ago and rejoiced greatly on the occasion he preached for my father in Columbus, Ohio. I marvel at the success and growth of the "Faith Message" and in the 45 countries that I have visited personally have failed to find even one where your efforts for Christ remain fruitless. Three years ago, I sat on the platform with T.L. Osborne at the winter meeting and your father laid hands on me and I was completely healed of an injury I received in the Virgin Islands. After three surgeries, I was completely free from pain for the first time in five years.

Appendix A

The purpose of this letter is in the interest of the Kingdom of God and a present danger that threatens to seriously further divide the Body of Christ along racial lines for years to come.

My personal ministry involves pastoring in the inner city of Chicago for the last 23 years. We were privileged to build the largest multi-ethnic city church in the United States. Through the years I've developed an understanding of and appreciation for the Afro-American perspective. Weekly I meet with Reverend Jesse Jackson and judges and community leaders in Chicago. Our cross-cultured activities have enriched our lives immeasurably, not the least of which is a beautiful eight-year-old grandson, whose other grandfather is black.

My heart sank last night when I viewed Fred Price's program on television and was apprised of the rift between your ministry and Fred Price's marvelous following.

This is to encourage you to take a courageous step of action that I feel could bring healing to the whole situation. Without doubt Fred Price is a man of God and a man of integrity who, if approached in sincerity and humility, would prove more than willing to respond positively.

I believe that the proper course of action would necessitate a sincere apology by you on radio, television and in print. Dr. C.M. Ward provided me with some invaluable personal advice many years ago. He said, "Any pastor who wants to remain at his post for a number of years needs to learn to eat crow publicly at least twice a year whether he needs it or not." With all due respect, in this situation, you need it.

Your apologetic statement as replayed by Rev. Price was tantamount to no apology at all. The flippant and trite way you chose to deal with the problem was a slap in the face, and remember these observations are from a white preacher.

As I see it, you have four options available to you:

1. Ignore the problem and hope that it goes away; it won't.

2. Admit that you were sincere in your observation and try to back them up with Scripture; unfortunately, you can't.

3. Admit that you were coerced into making your observation under pressure and that you really didn't believe them. Did you?

4. Confess that at the time you made the observation, you felt justified in doing so, but in retrospect realize that they were unjustified, unscriptural and insensitive.

You could then admonish the Body of Christ to racial unity and genuine repentance. We all know that in the economy of the Gospel the middle wall of hostility that separated the races has succumbed to the power of the cross.

From my view this last option is, in reality, your only option. I fear that if you choose to ignore this, in the interest of business as usual, the Body of Christ will suffer needlessly for years.

In the interest of the Kingdom,
[Pastor A]
Chicago, Illinois

As of the time this book is being published, I still have not heard from the minister on the tape. I had hoped that Pastor A's letter, coming as it does from another white person, might be more effective in reaching the minister and his father than mine had been. But it was not.

I want to thank all the people who wrote to me expressing their opinions on my communication with the ministry that made the tape, and on my teachings on race, religion and racism. Some of the response has been in support of what I've said and done, some has been critical, all of it has been deeply felt—because the subject of racism is one that most of us have passionate responses to, one way or the other.

An important part of eliminating racism and healing the wounds that have been created by it is to talk about our views openly, and to be open to examining them in the light of day and comparing them to the Word of God and the findings of science. Everyone who wrote to me has been courageous enough to share his or her opinions and experiences in an open manner, and to participate in the dialogue with me. That is why I appreciate your efforts.

As Pastor A suggests in his fax to the minister on the tape, I am waiting to respond positively whenever the minister is ready to recant and repent of what he said on the tape. I yearn to see our ministries once again united, as I yearn to see racism eliminated from the Body of Christ and for every one of every race to live with the knowledge of what God has told us: that we are all of one flesh and one blood, and that inside the dust of our flesh bodies we are all spirits created in the image of God.

Bibliography

This bibliography is not a complete record of all the works and sources consulted in the researching and writing of this book. It only indicates the substance and range of reading upon which the ideas and text were formed and is intended to serve as a convenience for those who wish to pursue the study of this subject further.

Albu, Emily, J. William Frost, Howard Clark Kee, Carter Lindberg and Dana L. Robert, *Christianity: A Social and Cultural History* (New York: Prentice-Hall, Inc., 1998).

Anderson, Claud, *Black Labor, White Wealth: The Search for Power and Economic Justice* (Bethesda, Maryland: PowerNomics Corporation, 1994).

Anderson, Claud, "PowerNomics," Teaching Seminar, Crenshaw Christian Center, Los Angeles (August 28-30, 1997).

Anderson, Claud, "Vision Beyond the Dream Speech," Teaching Seminar, Crenshaw Christian Center, Los Angeles (December 14, 1996).

Anderson, James F., Laronistine Dyson and Tazinski Lee, "Ridding the African-American Community of Black Gang Proliferation," *Western Journal of Black Studies*, v. 20, no. 2 (Summer 1996).

Backer, John H., *The Decision to Divide Germany* (Durham, North Carolina: Duke University Press, 1978).

Bard, Mitchell G., *The Complete Idiot's Guide to World War II* (New York: Alpha Books, 1999).

Barnes, Albert, *The Church and Slavery* (Philadelphia: Parry & McMillan, 1857).

Barnes, Catherine, *Journey from Jim Crow: The Desegregation of Southern Transit* (New York: Columbia University Press, 1983).

Berry, Henry, "Abolition of Slavery," Speech to House of Delegates of Virginia, January 11, 1832, State of Virginia Archives.

Berry, Mary Frances and John W. Blassingame, *Long Memory: The Black Experience in America* (New York: Oxford University Press, 1982).

Bible: Parallel Reference Bible, King James Version/New King James Version (Nashville: Thomas Nelson Publishers, 1979, 1980, 1982, 1991).

"Black Jesus in Union City, NJ: 'The Passion Play' Stirs Community Racism," *Jet*, v. 91, no. 18 (October 14, 1996): 12-13.

Blackburn, Robin, *The Making of New World Slavery: From the Baroque to the Modern, 1492-1800* (New York: Verso, 1997).

Blassingame, John W., ed., *Slave Testimony: Two Centuries of Letters, Speeches, Interviews, and Autobiography* (Baton Rouge: Louisiana State University Press, 1977).

Blumberg, Rhoda Lois, *Civil Rights: The 1960s Freedom Struggle*, Rev. ed. (Boston: Twayne Publishers, 1991).

Bowen, David Warren, *Andrew Johnson and the Negro* (Knoxville: University of Tennessee Press, 1989).

Brown, Richard D. and Stephen G. Rabe, eds., *Slavery in American Society* (Lexington, Massachusetts: D.C. Heath & Co., 1976).

Butler, Jon and Harry S. Stout, *Religion in American History* (New York: Oxford University Press, 1998).

Butterfield, Fox, *All God's Children: The Bosket Family and the American Tradition of Violence* (New York: Alfred A. Knopf, 1995).

Calloway-Thomas, Carolyn and John Louis Lucaites, eds., *Martin Luther King, Jr., and the Sermonic Power of Public Discourse* (Tuscaloosa: University of Alabama Press, 1993).

Bibliography

Cartwright, Samuel A., "Report on the Diseases and Physical Peculiarities of the Negro Race," *New Orleans Medical and Surgical Journal.*

Charner, Ivan and Bryna Shore Fraser, "Youth and Work: What We Know, What We Don't Know, What We Need to Know" (New York: Commission on Work, Family and Citizenship, William T. Grant Foundation, 1989).

Chennault, Ronald E., Joe L. Kincheloe, Shirley R. Steinberg, and Nelson M. Rodrigues, eds., *White Reign: Deploying Whiteness in America* (New York: St. Martin's Press, 1998).

Clary, Johnny Lee, *Boys in the Hoods: One Man's Journey From Hatred to Love* (Bakersfield, California: Pneuma Life Publishing, 1995).

Curry, George E. and Michelle McCalope, "Reduced to a Photo: A Family's Torment After the Tragic Dragging Death in Jasper, Texas," *Emerge: Black America's Newsmagazine*, v. 10, no. 7 (May 1999).

Curry, Richard O., ed., *The Abolitionists: Reformers or Fanatics?* (New York: Holt, Rinehart & Winston, Inc., 1995).

Daniels, Roger, *The Decision to Relocate the Japanese Americans* (Malabar, Florida: Robert E. Krieger Publishing Company, 1975).

Davies, Alan, *Infected Christianity: A Study of Modern Racism* (Kingston and Montreal: McGill-Queen's University Press, 1988).

Davis, Abraham L. and Barbara Luck Graham, *The Supreme Court, Race, and Civil Rights* (Thousand Oaks: Sage Publications, Inc., 1995).

Davis, Angela Y., *Women, Race, and Class* (New York: Vintage Books, A division of Random House, 1983).

Douglass, Frederick, *My Bondage and My Freedom* (New York: Dover Publications, Inc., 1969).

Douglass, Frederick, *Narrative of the Life of Frederick Douglass* (New York: Dover Publications, Inc., 1995).

Edwards, I.E.S., *The Pyramids of Egypt* (New York: Penguin Books, 1947).

Ellsworth, Scott and John Hope Franklin, *Death in a Promised Land: The Tulsa Race Riot of 1921* (Baton Rouge: Louisiana State University Press, 1982).

Engelman, Robert, "Geneticist: We're All From Africa," Science & Technology, *Scripps Howard News Service*.

Farwell, Byron, *Stonewall: A Biography of General Thomas J. Jackson* (New York: W.W. Norton & Co., Inc., 1992).

Finkenbine, Roy E., "Culture and Religion in the Quarters," in *Sources of the African-American Past: Primary Sources in American History* (New York: Longman Publishers, Inc., 1997).

Frederickson, George M., *White Supremacy: A Comparative Study in American & South African History* (New York: Oxford University Press, 1981).

Godolphin, R. B., ed., and George Rawlinson, trans., "Persian Wars," Book 2, *The Greek Historians: The Complete and Unabridged Historical Works of Herodotus, Thucydides, Xenophon, and Arrian* (New York: Random House, 1942).

Goings, Michael, *Free at Last? The Reality of Racism in the Church* (Shippensburg, Pennsylvania: Treasure House, an imprint of Destiny Image Publishers, Inc., 1995).

"Good Move In Dixie: Governor Says Strike Flag," *USA Today*, Final ed., News Section (December 2, 1996).

Hadjor, Kofi Buenor, *Dictionary of Third World Terms* (New York: Penguin Books, 1993).

Hale-Benson, Janice E., *Black Children: Their Roots, Culture, and Learning Styles* (Baltimore: Johns Hopkins University Press, 1986).

Bibliography

Ham, Ken, Andrew Snelling and Carl Wieland, *The Answers Book: Answers to the 12 Most-Asked Questions on Genesis and Creation/Evolution*, Rev. ed. (Green Forest, Arkansas: Master Books, Inc., 1993).

Hawkin, Walter L., *African American Biographies: Profiles of 558 Current Men and Women* (Jefferson, North Carolina: McFarland, 1992).

Herenstein, Richard and Charles Murray, *The Bell Curve* (New York: Free Press Paperbacks, 1996).

Hill, Samuel S., *Encyclopedia of Religion in the South* (USA: Mercer University Press, 1984).

Hood, Robert E., *Begrimed and Black: Christian Traditions on Blacks and Blackness* (Minneapolis: Fortress Press, 1994).

Hotz, Robert Lee, "Scientists Say Race Has No Biological Basis," *Los Angeles Times*, Home ed. (Monday, February 20, 1995): A-1.

"How Psychiatry Lit the Racial Fires," in *Creating Racism: Psychiatry's Betrayal* (Los Angeles: Citizens Commission on Human Rights, May, 1996): 4-7.

Kivel, Paul, *Uprooting Racism: How White People Can Work for Racial Justice* (New Gabriola Island, British Columbia: New Society Publishers, 1996).

Knowles, Elizabeth, ed., *The Oxford Dictionary of Phrase, Saying and Quotation* (New York: Oxford University Press, 1997).

Lehner, Mark, *The Complete Pyramids* (New York: Thames and Hudson, 1997).

"Life: Complexity and Organization," *Encyclopedia Americana*, International ed., v. 17 (Danbury, Connecticut: Grolier Limited, 1979): 418.

"Life: Evolution of Life," *Encyclopedia Americana*, International ed., v. 17 (Danbury, Connecticut: Grolier Limited, 1979): 424.

Mbali, Zolile, *The Churches and Racism: A Black South African Perspective* (London: SCM Press Ltd., 1987).

McKenzie, Steven L., *All God's Children: A Biblical Critique of Racism* (Louisville, Kentucky: Westminster John Knox Press, 1997).

Melton, J. Gordon, Larry G. Murphy and Gary L. Ward, *Encyclopedia of African American Religions* (New York: Garland Publishing, Inc., 1993).

Merida, Kevin, "On the Hill, Reparations Finds Few Supporters," *Emerge: Black America's Newsmagazine*, v. 8, no. 4 (February 1997): 26-27.

Miller, John Chester, *The Wolf by the Ears: Thomas Jefferson and Slavery* (Charlottesville, Virginia: University Press of Virginia, 1991).

Mullane, Deirdre, ed., *Crossing the Danger Water: Three Hundred Years of African-American Writing* (New York: Anchor Books Doubleday, 1993).

Noll, Mark A., *Religion and American Politics: From the Colonial Period to the 1980s* (New York: Oxford University Press, 1990).

Otabil, Mensa, *Beyond the Rivers of Ethiopia: A Biblical Revelation on God's Purpose for the Black Race* (Bakersfield, California: Pneuma Life Publications, 1993).

"Psychiatric Oppression of African Americans," in *Creating Racism: Psychiatry's Betrayal* (Los Angeles: Citizens Commission on Human Rights, May, 1996): 8-9.

Range, Peter Ross, "Interview with William J. Bennett," *Modern Maturity*, v. 38, no. 2 (March-April, 1995): 26, 30, 78.

Reiss, Oscar, *Blacks in Colonial America* (North Carolina: McFarland & Company, Inc. 1997).

"Religious Denominations in South Carolina Confess to Sin of Racism," *Jet*, v. 92, no. 3 (June 9, 1997): 27.

Rensberger, Boyce, "Horizons: Forget the Old Labels: Here's a New Way to Look at Race," *Washington Post*, no. 346 (November 16, 1994).

Robinson, Calvin R., Redman Battle and Edward W. Robinson, Jr., *The Journey of the Songhai People* (Philadelphia: Farmer Press, 1987).

Robinson, Cedric J., *Black Movements in America* (New York: Routledge, 1997).

Robinson, Lori, "Righting a Wrong: Commission to Study Reparation Proposals for African Americans," *Emerge: Black America's Newsmagazine*, v. 8, no. 4 (February 1997): 43-49.

Rogers, J.A., *From "Superman" to Man*, 5th ed. (St. Petersburg, Florida: Helga M. Rogers, 1968; reprint 1989).

Rogers, J.A., *Sex and Race: Negro-Caucasian Mixing in All Ages and All Lands*, v. I, 9th ed. (St. Petersburg, Florida: Helga M. Rogers, 1967).

Rogers, J.A., *Sex and Race: A History of White, Negro, and Indian Miscegenation in the Two Americas*, v. II (St. Petersburg, Florida: Helga M. Rogers, 1970).

Rogers, J.A., *Sex and Race: Why White and Black Mix in Spite of Opposition*, v. III, 5th ed. (St. Petersburg, Florida: Helga M. Rogers, 1944; reprint, 1972).

Ross, Leon T. and Kenneth A. Mimms, *African American Almanac: Day-by-Day Black History* (Jefferson, North Carolina: McFarland, 1997).

Salley, Columbus and Ronald Behm, *What Color Is Your God? Black Consciousness and the Christian Faith*, Carol Publishing Group ed. (New York: Citadel Press, 1995).

Salzman, Jack, David Lionel Smith and Cornel West, eds., *Encyclopedia of African American Culture and History* (New York: MacMillan Library Reference, 1996).

Santayana, George, "The Life of Reason," in Elizabeth Knowles, ed., *The Oxford Dictionary of Phrase, Saying, and Quotation* (New York: Oxford University Press, 1997).

"Scriptures for America Worldwide," Website address: pastor @christianidentity.org, last updated 2/20/95.

Stampp, Kenneth M., *The Peculiar Institution: Slavery in the Ante-Bellum South* (New York: Vintage Books, 1964).

Strong, James, *The New Strong's Exhaustive Concordance of the Bible*, Nelson's Comfort Print ed. (Nashville: Thomas Nelson Publishers, 1995).

Tierney, John, Lynda Wright and Karen Springen, "The Search for Adam and Eve," *Newsweek*, v. 109, no. 2 (January 11, 1988): 46-52.

Uniform Crime Reports for the United States, 1997 (Washington, D.C.: Federal Bureau of Investigation, U.S. Department of Justice, 1999).

Weisbord, Robert G., *Genocide? Birth Control and the Black American* (New York: Greenwood Press, The Two Continents Publishing Group. Ltd.)

"When Love Crosses the Line," Letters to the Editor, *Charisma*, v. 21, no. 1 (August 1995): 8.

Wilson, Carter A., *Racism: From Slavery to Advanced Capitalism* (Thousand Oaks, California: Sage Publications, 1996).

Wynes, Charles E., ed., *The Negro in the South Since 1865: Selected Essays in American Negro History* (Tuscaloosa: University of Alabama Press, 1971).

Index

The italicized n following page numbers refers to information to be found in footnotes; nn refers to more than one footnote on a page.

Index

Scriptural Index

All biblical quotes are taken from the New King James Version unless otherwise noted.

About the Author

Apostle Frederick K.C. Price is the founder of Crenshaw Christian Center (CCC) in Los Angeles, California. He began CCC in 1973, and shepherded it through 35 years into a ministry of world renown, with services held since 1989 in the 10,000-seat FaithDome.

In 1978, Apostle Price received instruction from God to begin a television broadcast. As a result, *Ever Increasing Faith Ministries* (EIFM) was launched, appearing initially in five of the nation's big-city television markets. Since that time, the broadcast has become global, and EIFM can be viewed on 132 stations in all 50 states and in six foreign countries. The broadcast is also heard on 15 radio programs and 19 Internet broadcast stations. Additionally, it can be seen on most social media platforms, including Facebook, Twitter, Instagram, YouTube, Pinterest, and others.

In 1990, Apostle Price founded the Fellowship of Inner-City Word of Faith Ministries (FICWFM), now renamed the Fellowship of International Christian Word of Faith Ministries. And in 2001, he established an East Coast church—Crenshaw Christian Center East in New York's Manhattan borough.

A visionary and widely respected teacher, he is the author of some 50 books on faith, healing, prosperity, the Holy Spirit and other subjects. His book, *How Faith Works,* is a recognized classic on the operation of faith and its life-changing principles. He has also authored three historic volumes under the title of *Race, Religion & Racism.* Apostle Price has sold more than 2.1 million books since 1976. His most recent works include, *Prosperity: Good News for God's People* and *Answered Prayer Guaranteed: The Power of Praying with Faith.*

Although Apostle Price had already begun operating under the mantle of apostle, in 2008 he was publicly affirmed as an apostle of faith. Under his gift as teacher, he established several schools for ministry and formal education on the grounds of CCC. Among them are Frederick K. C. Price III Christian Schools (preschool to 12th grade); the Ministry Training Institute; the CCC Correspondence School; the Frederick K.C. Price School of the Bible, and in 2008, the Apostle Price Ministry Training Center. Over the years, Apostle Price has received many prestigious awards—most notably, the Horatio Alger Award from the Horatio Alger Association of Distinguished Americans and the Southern Christian Leadership Council's Kelly Miller Smith Interfaith Award, both in 1978.

Apostle Price holds an honorary doctorate of divinity from Oral Roberts University in Tulsa, Oklahoma, and an honorary diploma from Rhema Bible Training Center in Broken Arrow, Oklahoma.

A year after his affirmation as apostle, and after more than 35 years as pastor, Apostle Price stepped aside to formally install his son, Frederick K. Price Jr., as pastor. He is currently the presiding prelate of CCC West and East, and serves at the helm as the chairman of CCC's board of directors. Apostle Price not only ministers in the FaithDome, but travels the world, mostly in the United States, teaching the uncompromising Word of God.

A devoted husband, Apostle Price has been married to Dr. Betty Price for 61 years. They are the proud parents of four children, and have 10 grandchildren, and four great-grandchildren.

Books by Apostle Frederick K.C. Price

HOW FAITH WORKS

RACE, RELIGION & RACISM, VOLUME 1
A Bold Encounter With Division in the Church

RACE, RELIGION & RACISM, VOLUME 2
Perverting the Gospel to Subjugate a People

RACE, RELIGION & RACISM, VOLUME 3
Jesus, Christianity and Islam

THE CHRISTIAN FAMILY
Practical Insight for Family Living

HOW TO OBTAIN STRONG FAITH
Six Principles

THE HOLY SPIRIT
The Helper We All Need

INTEGRITY
The Guarantee for Success

PROSPERITY
Good News for God's People

LIVING IN HOSTILE TERRITORY
A Survival Guide for the Overcoming Christian

ANSWERED PRAYER GUARANTEED

FAITH, FOOLISHNESS, OR PRESUMPTION?

THE POWER OF POSITIVE CONFESSION
Develop a Habit of Speaking Life, Not Death!

IDENTIFIED WITH CHRIST:
A Complete Cycle From Defeat to Victory

DR. PRICE'S GOLDEN NUGGETS
A Treasury of Wisdom for Both Ministers and Laypeople

FIVE LITTLE FOXES OF FAITH

THE CHASTENING OF THE LORD

TESTING THE SPIRITS

BEWARE! THE LIES OF SATAN

THE WAY, THE WALK,
AND THE WARFARE OF THE BELIEVER
A Verse-by-Verse Study on the Book of Ephesians

THREE KEYS TO POSITIVE CONFESSION

THE PROMISED LAND
A New Era for the Body of Christ

A NEW LAW FOR A NEW PEOPLE

THE VICTORIOUS, OVERCOMING LIFE
A Verse-by-Verse Study on the Book of Colossians

PRACTICAL SUGGESTIONS FOR SUCCESSFUL MINISTRY

LIVING IN THE REALM OF THE SPIRIT

THE HOLY SPIRIT
The Missing Ingredient

IS HEALING FOR ALL?

GROWING IN GOD'S WORD:
Devotional & Prayer Journal

Minibooks

THE TRUTH ABOUT ... THE BIBLE

THE TRUTH ABOUT ... DEATH THE

TRUTH ABOUT ... DISASTERS

THE TRUTH ABOUT ... FATE

THE TRUTH ABOUT ... FEAR

THE TRUTH ABOUT ... HOMOSEXUALITY

THE TRUTH ABOUT ... RACE

THE TRUTH ABOUT ... WORRY

THE TRUTH ABOUT ... GIVING

NOW FAITH IS

HOW TO BELIEVE GOD FOR A MATE

THANK GOD FOR EVERYTHING?

CONCERNING THOSE WHO HAVE FALLEN ASLEEP

THE ORIGIN OF SATAN

Specialty-size Books

WALKING IN GOD'S WORD
Through His Promises

WORDS OF WISDOM: WOW!

BUILDING ON A FIRM FOUNDATION

HOMOSEXUALITY:
State of Birth or State of Mind?

Spanish Books

COMO CREER EN DIOS PARA ENCONTRAR TU PAREJA

EDIFICANDONOS SOBRE UNA BASE FIRME
Una guia para el Desarrollo de Su Cristiana

To receive Apostle Price's book and tape catalog, or be placed on the EIF mailing list, please call:

(800) 927-3436

Apostle Price's books are also available at some local bookstores.

For more information, please write:

Crenshaw Christian Center
P.O. Box 90000
Los Angeles, CA 90009

or check your local TV or Webcast listing:

Ever Increasing Faith Ministries

or visit our Websites:

www.faithdome.org
www.faithdome.tv